HOW COME YOU CAN'T IDENTIFY YOUR KEY CUSTOMERS?

THE ESSENTIAL GUIDE TO KEY ACCOUNT SELECTION

PETER CHEVERTON

KOGAN PAGE

First published in Great Britain in 2002 by Kogan Page Limited entitled *If You're So Brilliant… How Come You Can't Identify Your Key Customers?*

Reissued in 2005 entitled *How Come You Can't Identify Your Key Customers?*

Kogan Page Limited
120 Pentonville Road
London N1 9JN
United Kingdom

British Library Cataloguing in Publication Data

A CIP record for this book is available from the British Library.

ISBN 0 7494 3729 4

Typeset by Saxon Graphics Ltd, Derby
Printed and bound in Great Britain by Bell & Bain Ltd, Glasgow

Contents

Introduction – to begin at the beginning

'You don't choose your key accounts, they choose you.'

Unforgivable fatalism or pragmatic wisdom?

On the side of wisdom is the fact that you can't impose key account management on a customer, the customer has to want and to allow your extra intentions. To ignore this is to tread the path of ever increasing frustration and ever diminishing returns. The practice of key account management requires a certain mutuality of outlook between supplier and customer – and to this degree the customer has a big hand in the choosing.

If that were the end of it, there would be no need for this book. The answer would be to sit back and wait for whichever customers 'call you forward'. There are two problems with such an approach, both serious enough to warrant the charge of unfor-givable fatalism. First, in the hubbub of competitive activity the customers may just not get around to calling you. Second, those that do call may not be the ones you most desire. In business, as in life, tales of 'star-crossed lovers' are mostly just that, tales.

GETTING THE RESOURCES RIGHT

If you are intent on practising key account management in your business, then the process of identification and selection is one of the most important you will undertake. Key account management almost always involves devoting an unequal share of limited resources to a relatively small number of customers. This must mean taking resources from others. This is not something to get wrong, but backing the wrong horse is surprisingly easy, particularly when the only guide to form is last year's races.

Backing the right horses...

One of my favourite key account managers once said to me that the main qualification he required was 'a degree in horse racing'. He went on to say that he had the gut feel already but would appre-ciate some help with turning it into something a little more acceptable to his bosses.

If your marketplace is so dynamic, or for that matter, to take the other extreme, so homogeneous, that you can't safely distinguish one customer from another in terms of their importance in the future, then devoting an unequal share of resources to any selected group will be a very risky activity. What you gain with the chosen few you may lose with the others, and learning that you did indeed back the wrong horses always comes too late to change your mind, still less your commitments.

Of course, if there really is no way to distinguish one customer from another, then perhaps key account management is not the solution. In such an event the old fashioned 'milk round' approach may be safer, treating all customers as equally deserving of time and attention. Or there is the more aggressive 'hunter-killer' approach – where you allow short-term success to determine your future – maybe that might work out better for you. But in either case we are perhaps back in the area of unfor-givable fatalism. It is a rare market indeed where there are no clues to indicate the relative importance of customers, and an incurably, not to say stub-bornly, short-sighted business that can't find a set of criteria to sharpen that focus.

GETTING EVERYONE TO AGREE

Perhaps you already think you know your key accounts, maybe you are certain, but if you are honest, isn't there still one problem? You are clear, but the rest of your business doesn't seem to see it your way.

This is in fact a major problem, a killer. The management of key accounts demands a cross- func-tional, cross-business, cross-regional approach. All must share the objectives, all must contribute the resources, and all must channel their functional expertise towards the goal of customer satisfaction. None of this will happen if there is disagreement on who those key customers are.

The tale of the innocent sales rep

I learned this lesson in the first few months of my selling career. I sold decorative paint to independent retailers, and as an eager young rep out in rural East Anglia – where I was warned there would be little I could do to rouse customers from their comfortable slumber – I determined to identify those customers worthy of the most attention, my key accounts. After poring over my sales statistics and pushing pins of different colours into a map of my territory I went off to inform my local distribution depot, absolutely certain of my analysis.

For 10 minutes or so I briefed them on the key accounts that they must now give extra attention to, and then reeled with amazement as they contradicted almost every customer identified. For me, a sales rep, a key account was one where I could expect a large order as the result of my call. For my distribution colleagues this was the sin of sending eager young reps out in the first place! For them, a key account was a customer so regular and so consistent in their order pattern that they could form the backbone of their workload planning.

We agreed to differ and I went away wiser on one very important issue – it was highly unlikely that key accounts could be identified by single criteria and certainly not from the narrow perspective of any one function. Fortunately, I was dealing with rather small independent retailers in a quiet corner of the country, not the global customers that might have determined our whole future. There is a time to learn by your mistakes, and a time to get it right.

So, just as important as a means of identifying the key customers is a means of communicating the choice to all concerned and aligning their activities in order to manage these accounts to their full potential.

This book sets out a 10-step process and it is significant that only three of these steps (6, 7 and 8) are devoted to the actual mechanics of selection. The other seven are concerned with setting the context, preparing the ground and securing business-wide support. If you are tempted to jump straight in and skip these seven steps, then I can only warn you that what you think you are gaining in speed at the outset will be more than counterbalanced by the time wasted in frustrated and thwarted application, not to mention the costs of getting it wrong.

Figure 0.1 illustrates the importance of planning by suggesting the outcome of over-hasty, unthinking and unilateral decisions.

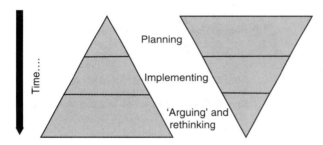

Figure 0.1   The importance of planning

The less time given to planning, the more time required for rethinking when it goes wrong. Here's a challenge to you; if you think that you haven't got the time for all this 'background' stuff, then where are you going to find the time to do it all again when it fails to take? In this matter, to begin at the beginning was never better advice.

Failing to plan is planning to fail

THE 10 STEPS

Figure 0.2 (page 6) shows the 10-step process as a flow chart, indicating that while the steps do form a broadly linear process, there are several points at which you will need to go back to some earlier decisions, using your steadily increasing knowledge and

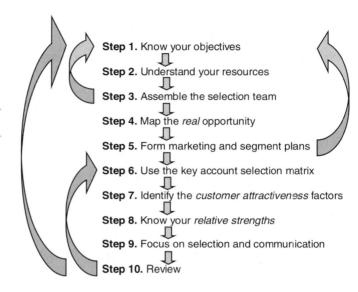

The 10 steps

Step 1. Know your objectives
⇩
Step 2. Understand your resources
⇩
Step 3. Assemble the selection team
⇩
Step 4. Map the *real* opportunity
⇩
Step 5. Form marketing and segment plans
⇩
Step 6. Use the key account selection matrix
⇩
Step 7. Identify the *customer attractiveness* factors
⇩
Step 8. Know your *relative strengths*
⇩
Step 9. Focus on selection and communication
⇩
Step 10. Review

Figure 0.2   The 10 steps

your widening team of experts, to challenge some of the assumptions behind those decisions.

This is of course a good thing, and it does allow you to make a start somewhere without prejudicing all future decisions. Some would argue, and with much justification, that you should start with Step 5 – the marketing plan and market segmentation – or perhaps Step 3 – the assembly of a project team. Either is fine, if you wish it so, provided that you really do start with a clear marketing plan, or that a project team can easily be assembled as the first step in the process. Whatever the case, the flow chart will take you back to Step 1 from either of those starting points.

Step 1

Your objectives

Step 1 involves asking what you want from key account management (KAM).

Before we go any further be sure of one thing – KAM involves a great deal of effort. A key account is an investment of your business's time and resources. It is an investment in your future and like all long-term investments it will require nurturing and protecting, often against onslaughts from within as well as without. That being so, you had best have some good reasons for pursuing this course.

KAM is not mandatory. If you really can achieve your business objectives without it, then you may be well advised to do so. Increasingly, however, it is being recognized as an essential component of business success.

A major investment... so what's the return?

To help you complete this first step we will start with a definition of KAM in its broadest terms, move on to an assessment of why it is becoming such an essential component of business success, and conclude with some examples of typical objectives.

A BROAD DEFINITION

1. For a carefully selected group of customers, develop a depth and breadth of relationship that goes well beyond a classic buyer/seller 'bow-tie' – to what we will call the 'diamond' relationship (described in Step 2).

   Too many companies call far too many customers key accounts – the result being no genuine key accounts at all.

2. Use the diamond relationship to acquire a thorough understanding of the customers' business, their markets, their objectives, their drivers, and their challenges.

   This goes well beyond the objectives of traditional selling, calling on skills of strategic thinking and analysis that may be absent even in your best salespeople.

3. Create genuinely added-value propositions that impact positively on the customer's objectives, drivers and challenges. Delivering these propositions may take you beyond your current capabilities.

   Developing new, and business-wide, capabilities is part of the responsibility of KAM.

4. Align your whole business behind implementing these propositions, so improving the quality of your total business.

    This is the hardest step of all – dealing with organizational issues and not least politics and egos – yet quite frankly if you can't achieve this fourth step in the process, you may be better off not starting out on the first three. Raising customer expectations only to disappoint them through your own internal inertia is usually worse than there being no expectations in the first place.

If you don't mean it... don't do it!

Why KAM matters, and why now

- Markets mature, competition gets hotter, and there is a tendency for suppliers to be increasingly commoditized.
- Gaining competitive advantage through products or technology gets ever harder, and for many it is no longer an option.
- Customers grow larger, more genuinely global, more complex, and more demanding.
- The growing sophistication of the purchasing role, particularly the way it has harnessed the potential of new e-tools, is sufficient to warrant the phrase a 'purchasing revolution'. There is need of a reaction from the supplier's side.

Recent years have seen a lot of things stacked in the buyer's favour, and KAM provides a rare opportunity to redress the balance towards the supplier, for some, perhaps the only opportunity.

If talk of 'redressing the balance' sounds rather one-sided, perhaps even confrontational, then that is not the intention. The intent is to find grounds for

KAM and an even 'balance of power'

partnership, not confrontation, but remember, without a fairly even 'balance of power' at the outset, partnership will look like humbug from one perspective and unnecessary from the other. If the notion of partnership is 'forced' in such a circumstance, then in practice it can hardly be expected to be a partnership of equals.

Figure 1.1 illustrates the shift in the 'balance of power' and indicates how key account management may serve to redress it. Notice that to do this, 'buyer' and 'seller' have been replaced by 'customer' and 'supplier', a comment on the need for a cross-functional team sell from a fully aligned business.

The relationship – a 'secret' source of competitive advantage

I was asked quite recently by a new client if they could speak with some of my existing clients to gain ideas on how to go about implementing a KAM strategy in their own business. To my surprise (though really I shouldn't have been surprised) many of my clients were very reluctant to discuss this aspect of their business, even though the new client was in no way a competitor. The point was clear – KAM has made the nature of the customer relationship a vital component of competitor advantage and the owners of this advantage are as reluctant to share their secrets as they would have been to divulge product formulations or patented technologies, or to give cost breakdowns.

POSSIBLE OBJECTIVES

Examples of other people's objectives should be treated with care. Your own objectives will of course be quite unique to your own business circumstances, and indeed if they are not, then they are perhaps too vague to be truly useful. Like all good

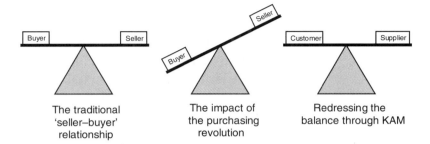

Figure 1.1   Shift in the balance of power

objectives they should adhere to the SMART acronym, as shown in Figure 1.2.

It has to be said that an uncomfortably large proportion of business objectives fail this simple test. Take a moment to try your own out against it – how do they fare?

Your objectives for KAM should of course follow on from your overall business objectives, and even more critically they should respond to the particular challenges and opportunities of your own business environment.

- **S**pecific
- **M**easurable
- **A**chievable
- **R**elevant
- **T**imed

Figure 1.2   The SMART acronym

The nature of your objectives will of course determine your choice of key accounts. It will also influence the way in which you practise KAM and that will in itself have a bearing on your final selection. Clarity at this stage is vital.

Shown below are six typical objectives for KAM. In each case an example of how this objective may be focused by a particular business circumstance is given (some are 'smarter' than others) and a comment is made on what such an objective may entail for the business – a suggestion, if you like, of what KAM might feel like in each case:

How it feels

- The retention of existing business and customers in a competitive environment.

  To reduce the defection rate of existing business with our key accounts (measured as products or projects 'owned', but lost to the competition) from 10 per cent (current year) to less than 5 per cent per year within two years. This halving of our defection rate will double the lifetime value of these products and projects.

  Retention

  If retention is your goal, then clearly existing customers will form your key accounts and the practice of KAM will be to build barriers to entry by competitors or alternative solutions. This should not be mistaken for a negative approach – the best way to build barriers is to get in first and to propose the new ideas yourself. Constant vigilance – 'knowing every mouse that crawls across the customer's warehouse floor', as my first sales manager used to say – will therefore be a particular characteristic of this style of KAM. As business exists already, the team involved may be quite large.

  Building barriers

- To **grow** through winning entry into new customers.

  To secure three new long-term contracts, each of a minimum value of US $1 million, with targeted customers in the European pharmaceutical market within the next two years.

  Key accounts will often be customers that are as yet no more than targets. This is a long-term challenge with the initial investment taking some time to pay off. A significant task will be finding ways to overcome the barriers to entry placed in your way by existing suppliers. A particular characteristic of this style of KAM is exploration and research. An entrepreneurial spirit in the key account team will be a real advantage, perhaps a must. As such penetration strategies must be carefully controlled, the 'up-front' team may be quite small at the outset.

- To manage **global** or **regional** customers with a consistent style and appropriate proposition.

  To achieve a global 'preferred supplier' status, as defined by our customer's vendor ratings, effective in all territories with our identified global key accounts, to be achieved to a timescale in line with our customer's global organization plans.

  The key accounts will not simply be those that have a global presence, but those that work in a genuinely global or regional manner, with expectations of consistency and uniformity across all their operations. This style of key account management will call on senior-level commitment, probable senior-level involvement, and possible structural reorganization. It will also

Growth

Overcoming barriers

Global aproach

From the top down

require excellent communication tools and skills across territorial boundaries. The team will be spread around the world, with all the concomitant pros and cons of different languages and time zones and the complexities of cultural diversity.

● To manage customers serviced by **multiple business units** from our own company, with a consistent style and appropriate proposition.

To ensure a fully coordinated and consistent management of the relationship and proposition with key accounts serviced by more than one of our business units. To establish a key account manager in each case with full authority to act on cross-business issues, and to be measured by a composite profit and loss account for the customer.

Multi-business consistency...

This is a particularly challenging task as the chances are that your business unit structure has grown up such that each unit can operate independently of the others. This has many advantages, particularly in a complex company with a breadth of different products, markets and technologies, until it comes to servicing key accounts that want to deal with more than one business unit. Success will demand some robust cross-business processes and disciplines, as well as a commitment from the very top. The team will be a complex one, calling on all the skills of working in a matrix structure.

... across business lines

One of the biggest challenges in such a scenario is knowing when to act. There will be a time, when viewed from the supplier's side, when a concerted effort looks to have some advantages, but perhaps the efforts involved are too great – the return on the investment will be poor. At what point does the switch-over occur? The answer to this must come from the customer's perspective. At what point does the customer see benefit from receiving a concerted sales approach? That is the moment to be ready for.

- The creation of a **customer intimate** business, driven by the demands of its key accounts.

  Over a period of two years to transform the objectives and operating procedures of each function within our business so that they align to clearly identified requirements as agreed with our key customers.

  Customer intimacy...

  This is certainly the vaguest of the six objectives listed here, but in the end it may prove to be the longest lasting. It will lead to the involvement of a wide range of functions and departments in the process of customer contact and management in order to ensure that functional excellence is defined by customer-focused criteria. In the end, each key account may become regarded as a kind of business unit or individual market segment.

  ... from all functions and departments

- The achievement of **operational excellence** through grouping and managing customers that have similar trading requirements – key accounts (full service), transactional accounts (simple offers), opportunistic accounts (spot deals), etc.

  To improve operational efficiencies (manufacturing, distribution, customer service) by developing a clear and compact range of 'best value for money' propositions, packaged for specific account types.

  Operational excellence...

**... in pursuit of
competitive advantage**

While the language may sound like market segmentation, this is the most internally focused of the six objectives. This is not necessarily wrong, provided that the market circumstances allow competitive advantage to be gained in such a way. The practice of key account management would be highly standardized in such an environment, with processes taking precedent over customer intimacy.

Of course, in your own business the objectives may combine any or all of the above. Be aware, however, that the more complex the objectives the more challenging the task of KAM. For one customer the objective may be retention, and this, as has been shown, calls for a particular style of KAM. For another customer the objective may be growth, requiring a quite different approach.

Mixing objectives within a business – retention and growth for instance – will require a subtle appreciation of the different styles of KAM and a very flexible management style. Take an even tougher mix of objectives, the challenge of managing global customers while servicing them from multiple business units, and you will almost certainly be looking towards some form of structural reorganization.

The kind of objectives discussed here are not those of a traditional sales approach. They do not focus on quarterly targets or annual budgets. They are the business-wide objectives for the practice of KAM and will determine the allocation of resources and the activities of all functions, not just sales. They will

Application exercise

Before moving on to Step 2, take some time to note your objectives for KAM. It is quite likely that you will want to revise these after progressing through later steps in the process, but rather than 'suspending judgement' try here to be bold.

Managing the future (and this is the purpose of KAM) is about achieving a realistic balance between your objectives, the market opportunity, and the resources you can apply. Step 2 will help you think more about the resources, and Steps 4 and 5 the market opportunity.

So, what do you want?

require business-wide acceptance and business-wide support.

Step 2

Your resources

At this point you need to ask; how far can you take this, and with how many customers? The type of objectives you set for KAM will determine the type of relationships you seek to develop, and will indicate with how many customers you may wish to do this. But objectives do not exist in a vacuum, there is also the not insignificant matter of resources.

It has already been indicated that most businesses attempt to label too many customers as key accounts. The result is that none receive the particular attention required. Those customers that deserve it most and would thrive if it was received are under-resourced, and so plod on in a rather commonplace way. Those customers that were perhaps rather commonplace in the first instance but now receive the title of key account and some of the trappings, perform no better as a result. Here lies mediocrity, frustration, and disillusionment.

My experience in working with a wide range of clients has not led me to identify a perfect number of key accounts; this is far too business specific to be determined by any kind of industry average. It has, however, led me to conclude that whatever number the business thinks they can cope with at the outset almost always proves to be too many – very often twice as many as they ought to manage. Far better to work with a few, and to do it well, than to avoid the difficult decisions and end up doing it badly with all.

The vital few

In Step 2 we need to identify the extent to which we wish to take this targeted application of resources, always remembering that if we give more to some, it must come from others.

Let us consider three general approaches to selling, indicating some of the advantages and disadvantages of each and how they might be used in the pursuit of a KAM strategy. Our purpose in Step 2 is not to explain how to manage key accounts, simply to indicate what managing them might look and feel like in order to help us in our selection process.

THREE MODES OF 'SELLING'

Mode 1 – the milk round

In a perfect world the salesperson's house is right in the middle of their sales area, which is of course a perfect circle. The customers are spread with perfect symmetry around the sales area and the salesperson has an immaculate cloverleaf journey plan around it on six calls a day, working a four-week cycle, and with an amazingly low miles-per-call measure.

If this ever was a perfect world, then it is passing fast. For most of us it is gone already. The point about the milk round approach is that it thrives on order and efficiency. These days order and efficiency can be more easily attained by other means – enter the call centre, the telesales team, and the e-commerce system.

The milk round approach, whether in high- or low-tech guise, has very little to do with the management of key accounts, though it may be perfect for managing many of those customers not defined as key (See Step 6).

Its main advantage is that large numbers of customers can be managed with highly uniform service standards. Therein lies its main weakness for our purpose – the relative inability to recognize customers with extra potential and to do anything about that recognition. 'Come back tomorrow because you will learn something.' 'Sorry, I'll see you in another month when my perfect journey plan says you deserve some more of my attention.'

Having dwelt on an approach that is far from appropriate for KAM, let's deal with another that many still think is very appropriate – the hunter mode.

Mode 2 – the hunter

Figure 2.1 illustrates a typical, perhaps the most typical, sales relationship, what we might call the bow-tie relationship.

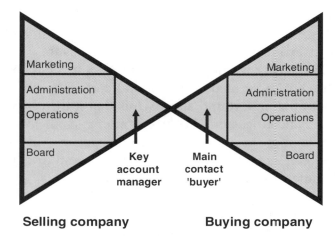

Figure 2.1 The 'bow-tie' relationship

This is the perfect arrangement for the hunter mode of selling.

Below are the main advantages and disadvantages of this mode:

- The salesperson has only one contact at the customer, which means that they can be in and out in no time, and so manage a large number of customers. The salesperson's own organization is nicely streamlined to receive the orders and make it all happen with great efficiency.

- In a market where there are lots of customers and there is rapid growth, the hunter approach may be just right. If you are a new entrant and seek quick penetration, then even more so. It can be very effective in the short term, particularly with an aggressive sales force, probably young, and driven by a well-designed commission package. Pharmaceutical companies with large sales teams with an average age of 25 can see an awful lot of doctors very quickly when a new drug is launched.

- The hunter approach is fun – at least the successful hunter will regard it as such, and when compared to the plod and the slog of the farmer (see below) who would want to change?

- The downside of the hunter mode is seen in the poor level of customer retention, not so serious while business is booming but of grave concern when the market opportunity reaches a more mature stage.

- There are all sorts of problems with the hunter approach when seeking to develop a customer relationship beyond the simple transaction of a product at a price.

- It lives for the moment – investment (our definition of a key account) is of little consequence to a sales person who is focused on this month's commission and may not plan to be on the team next year.

Investment, or jam today?

- It does not discriminate – a kill is a kill. Think of a real hunter, a lioness on the Serengeti Plain surveying the ever-moving herd of wildebeest. Does this lioness pick out the healthiest looking specimen, the one with the most meat and the longest eating potential, or does it prey on the sick and the weak?

- Communications with the customer are channelled through one point – great for control, not so good for acquiring a thorough understanding of the customer's business, their markets, their objectives, their drivers, and their challenges, and absolutely hopeless for creating genuine added-value propositions that impact positively on those objectives, drivers and challenges. (Remember our definition of KAM from Step 1.) And we should not even think of this approach as helping you to align your whole business behind implementing these propositions, so improving the quality of your total business.

This remains the model for the masses, not for the chosen few, the key accounts. For them, we must turn to the farmer mode of selling.

Mode 3 – the farmer

Figure 2.2 illustrates the sort of relationship that represents a farmer approach and indeed a KAM approach – we will call it the diamond relationship.

This is the sales approach that seeks to develop the customer's potential over time. Investment is

The 'diamond' relationship

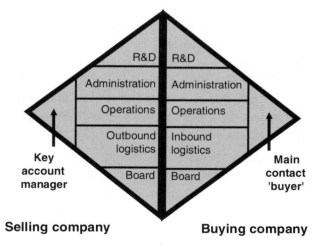

Figure 2.2   The 'diamond' relationship

the name of the game, whether for growth or retention, investing time and effort for a pay-off next year or even beyond. This long-term view encourages, indeed necessitates, broad and deep contacts with the customer, nurtured in anticipation of a future beyond today's sale. We are of course describing KAM, but it is not so easy to operate as might at first appear. Plenty of things can work against the farmer approach:

- short-term targets imposed from above;
- inappropriate commission or reward packages based on volume today;
- sales management that favours efficiency over effectiveness;
- the insistence that all customers are equal – you can't farm them all.

How many customers you can farm is not only a matter of your sales resource, it is dependent on the resources of the whole business. People in support functions will be involved more and more with the customer, and their very involvement will generate more activities and projects. If we stop to consider for a moment not textbook models but the reality of the business of selling – the continual demands from all quarters, the emergencies, the crises and the fire-fighting – when will you find the time to move away from the hunter mode and progress towards farmer-style diamonds?

Aim to do it well, and that means not overdoing it

And even if you do manage to find the time (and it will take plenty, be assured of that – two years is not a bad guess for a proper transition), the workload involved in such a transition period is perhaps higher than at any other time.

The answer to the question of how many customers you can farm just has to be not many.

Application exercise

Return to Step 1
If the reality of KAM is going to be something like the diamond relationship, with all its demands on people's time and its tendency to generate increasing levels of activity, then were the objectives we set for KAM achievable and realistic? Perhaps we need to revise our aims. Or perhaps we need to increase our resources instead. Whichever it is, take some time to rethink before proceeding to the next steps.

Focus, focus, and more focus
Steps 4–9 will show you how to focus your view, honing in on the real targets and resisting the temptation to use a shotgun approach. For now, just be resolved to focus

Step 3

Assemble the selection team

At the outset we said that this was not a simple linear process, and here comes our first serious hiccup – why not start with the team?

Good question, and in many a situation you should and would start there. I have assumed that you want to get a little ahead of the pack and to get your own thoughts together before involving others. Indeed, without your level of understanding, how would you know what sort of team was required, and what its purpose should be? Perhaps most of all, you wouldn't be so fully aware as you are by now of the absolute importance of a team. This is my best case for making it Step 3. If you can make a better one for making it Step 1, that's no problem.

Step 3 can be discussed quickly, but it is one of the longest of the steps to complete. It involves more than simply calling a meeting. It means gathering the right team of people to discuss and agree on one of the most important decisions you have to make in your business – which customers will get our closest attention?

Why do you need a team?

Don't even *think* of doing this on you own

For one, you can't possibly have the knowledge to carry out Step 3 alone. This is not a matter of pride or confidence, it is a simple observation that a business team will always know more than an individual. And secondly, do it alone and *you* might be pleased with the outcome, but you will soon find that dozens of *others* will disagree.

THE IDEAL TEAM

The ideal team is only ever ideal for the purpose for which it is formed. There is in fact a dual purpose for this team:

- to identify and select the key accounts based on a combination of intimate customer knowledge and a clear vision of future strategy and goals;
- to give that selection sufficient authority for it to mean something across the business (selection without implementation is meaningless).

We want to form the ideal team for this dual purpose, and it should not worry us that the team may be of little use for anything else.

There are three broad requirements, which will be expanded upon later:

- Ensure that there is sufficient authority to make the decisions stick. This is not always a question of seniority. Authority comes from status for sure, but also from the respect that an individual's (or a team's) opinions are granted. Make sure the team is constructed such that it will be respected. Aim to mix youthful enthusiasm with the experience of the 'grey hairs'. Aim to minimize the impact of the know-alls, the 'dyed in the wool', and the cynics. And after that last piece of advice, I just hope you have some folk left to construct this team…

- Ensure the right combination of vision and knowledge.

- Represent all of the functions that will be involved in managing and servicing these customers. Try to miss no one, but most of all don't miss that awkward lot who disagree with everyone else – they are just the bunch to bring it all crashing down, once you've made your decisions, if they were *not* involved. There are politics as well as principles to be looked to here.

How senior?

Take your time and get the right people. The identification and selection activity described in this book, if it is to mean anything in practice, is going to need support and commitment from the very top. So make sure you start there, whether it be seeking advice, winning support, arguing the case, or even finding active team members.

Should the Board be involved in such an exercise? It depends. Do they have sufficient knowledge? Are they close enough to the customers? I would put it differently. I would be worried if the Board were not very closely interested, if they were not urging the process on, and if they didn't want to ensure that the best people were involved in the process. I guess in an ideal world I would want all of that, and then hope that there was a group of people other than the Board who would actually make it happen – but then, of course, it depends...

Knowledge or vision?

Consider two scenarios. In the first, the team is a group of senior managers who approach the task very much with their eyes on the recently agreed five-year plan. 'Vision' abounds, but 'What', say the sales force, 'What do they know about **our** customers?'

In the second scenario, it is a group from sales and customer service that make up the selection team, and their efforts reflect their intimate knowledge of the customers. 'Fine', say the bosses, 'but what about **tomorrow's** customers? Where's the vision?'

There is another problem with a team of salespeople – everyone wants their customers to be rated as key accounts!

The ideal team must aim to combine vision and knowledge. Knowledge will exist in a lot of places and any attempt to gather it all together in one team would result in an unworkable monster. Perhaps the solution is a core team, probably with a bias towards 'vision', who call on the knowledge of others as and when it is required.

THE TEAM IN PRACTICE

These three broad guidelines are fine in theory but we must also consider the team in practice, complete with the personality clashes, the competing egos, the politics, and the shrinking violets who contribute nothing but in fact know all the answers. There is one simple, but rarely asked question – will the team work together?

The work of Dr Meredith Belbin provides us with some guidance here. Belbin proposes a model of nine key team roles (see Figure 3.1), where each role has a distinct and valuable contribution to make to the successful working of the whole team. The 'ideal' team might be said to contain all roles, but the

With acknowledgement to the work of Dr Meredith Belbin
Figure 3.1 'Belbin' team rules

specific purpose of the team may call for a more specific make-up.

A group of perfectly cloned, statistically minded analysts might get on well together, but they will never complete the task in hand. Similarly, a room full of hard-driving, objective-led extroverts might make a lot of appropriate sounding noise, but will they come to an agreed conclusion? No chance.

For the dual tasks of this particular team there are some essential 'Belbin' roles:

Coordinator

This is a complex task calling on knowledge and expertise across functions, businesses and regions.

Getting it together

Someone with the appropriate skills of diplomacy, facilitation and persuasion will be essential. Very often the team will call on the help of an outside consultant to fill this role.

Resource investigator

This is the person who goes out and finds things –

Finding it out

information, experts, assistance. Without such a role in the team the result could be very introspective, not to say based on heavy doses of navel gazing.

Monitor evaluator

Seen by some as slow and over cautious, these are the folk who keep you honest. They apply checks

Making sure you are sure

and balances and won't let you make rash decisions based on anecdotal or insufficient evidence.

Implementer

The steps proposed in this book represent a process, and the implementer's ability to comprehend and manage processes will be of great importance.

By highlighting these four roles I don't intend to diminish the others.

> **Shapers** will give direction and maintain momentum when things get tough.
>
> **Completer finishers** will ensure that you get things done (and there is a fair bit of nitty gritty in Steps 6–8).
>
> A **plant** will keep you on your toes, challenging accepted wisdoms.
>
> **Specialists** will provide the necessary expertise and knowledge.
>
> **Team workers** will hold you all together when you threaten to explode or fragment.

(For help on how to assess the 'Belbin' team roles and apply the model to your own team see Next Steps... at the end of this book.)

TEAM SIZE

Despite ensuring sufficient authority, vision and knowledge, having the right range of functions, and constructing the team with an eye on 'Belbin's' team role types, you must of course avoid a team of 20, or you will get nowhere fast. The ideal number? Well it doesn't have to be nine just because there are nine Belbin team roles. The contributions made by each team role type can be doubled up by individuals, or they can be regarded as ground rules for team behaviour – if you have no natural monitor evaluator, then the team must take care to ensure that it instigates its own checks and balances. Perhaps, as noted above, a core team of three or four can drive the process, calling on a wider circle of 'expert witnesses' as required, and reporting back to those occasional team members as progress is made.

The real answer to this question must depend on how important it is to bring the whole business in behind the process. Remember, the team is not only there to make the selection, but must have sufficient authority to make that selection mean something across the whole business.

CLARITY OF PURPOSE

Once the team is assembled make sure that everyone shares the same purpose. For this to be so they must all understand the issues and the challenges that accompany KAM. Get them all to read a good book, or better still, arrange for a facilitated workshop to get the task moving.

TIMETABLE

Give yourself a generous timetable, but also try to set firm deadlines for each step. Exact timings can only be based on your own circumstances – the size of your company, the nature of your business, the complexity of the market, your level of knowledge and the urgency of the outcome – but don't expect to finish in a week, and aim not to drag on for more than six months or so.

It is more important to do this properly than to do it quickly. Using 'Belbin' speak, the team's monitor evaluator should be 'keeping you honest'. Aiming to get through the whole process in a day or two will be a day or two wasted, and any outcomes are liable to be rather dangerous. In the end, this is one of those exercises that never does quite get completed, something is always changing out there – customers merge, competitors come and go, opportunities shift – so expect to be fully done some time never. Key accounts are not carved in stone for all time.

Expect to be done 'some time never'

Application exercise

Try to define your 'dream team':

What functions must be represented?

Who will provide the knowledge required?

How will it be accessed?

Who will provide the team skills and roles required?

Who will provide the necessary authority?

How many will be needed:
    to capture the knowledge required?
    to win business-wide support for the process?
    to make it happen?

Step 4

Mapping the opportunity

The selection of key accounts demands a narrowing of focus on to a handful of real 'winners', but there is a stage in the process of identification and selection when the focus should be widened rather than narrowed. Step 4 is the place to broaden the view.

There is a great danger that businesses choose their key accounts based on their most recent customer successes. Likewise, there is the sin of only looking at today's largest or most profitable. Given that this already means *yesterday's* largest or most profitable, we are at some risk of living up to that cliché, so beloved by management consultants, of driving our car by looking in the rear-view mirror.

Opportunities generally lie ahead, or in uncharted territory

It is very important then to take a fresh look at the market, just to be sure that things are not shifting in new, almost unnoticed directions. We will use a tool borrowed from marketing, the market map.

THE MARKET MAP

Use the market map to look for tomorrow's opportunities. This tool is a diagram showing the channels to market for your product or service. Nothing particularly broadening in that you might think, except that what we want to capture here are *all* the channels and *all* the influences playing on those channels. When salespeople map out the channels to market they tend to focus on those channels that represent the largest volumes and have been the most significant in the recent past.

Figure 4.1 shows such a map for a manufacturer of paint sold into the motor car repair or 'refinish' market, often referred to as the '*you bend 'em we mend 'em*' trade. We will follow this particular example through several levels of 'mapping sophistication', hoping to show how each additional level might effect your view of where the key accounts lie.

Build the map, level by level

With this view of the market it will be no surprise to find where the key accounts are looked for at first – among the paint distributors. The sales resource will have been allocated principally to pushing the product into and through these distributors.

In time an added sophistication might have been to look beyond the distributors to examine the opportunities in the body shops themselves. There may be scope for considering some of the larger chains as key accounts, managed jointly by the paint manufacturer and the distributor. Such joint responsibilities are never easy, and the paint manufacturer

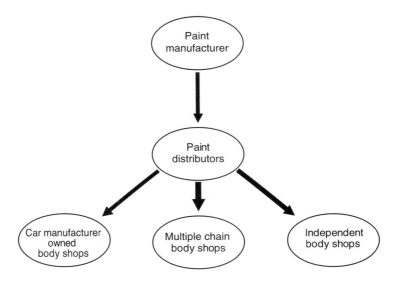

Figure 4.1   Market map for a manufacturer of paint

is probably conscious of playing second fiddle to the distributors' first violin. Another approach might be to highlight the OEM (original equipment manufacturer) body shops, but these don't necessarily form a coherent group, being a collection of independent, chain, franchised or OEM-owned operations – not promising territory for identifying key accounts.

Figure 4.2 adds an important new element to the map, the OEM, the car manufacturer.

The car manufacturer has an increasing interest in what goes on in the body shops that are part of its own service networks. Not only are there issues of customer care and quality control, but there are margins to be made. As profits from the sale of cars grow ever slighter, so the margins from after-sales service become ever more attractive. The car manufacturer's newly aroused interest is an opportunity

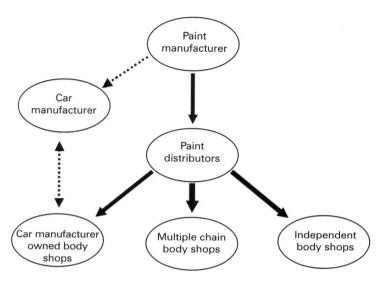

Figure 4.2 Market map including the car manufacturer

for the paint's supplier, a specification route for their product that bypasses the over-mighty distributor.

The possibility of regarding the car manufacturer as a key account begins to appear, even though the manufacturer buys nothing directly – the sale will still be made through the distribution network – but it is none the less a customer, and a hugely important focus of influence.

Figure 4.3 adds a part of the map that should really always have been there – market maps should always go down to the final consumer – but the historical power and grip of the distributors had rather obscured their importance.

With the addition of the end-consumer, whether in the form of the private motorist, the car hire firms, or the fleet management companies, we see a whole new dynamic emerge. The car manufacturer has a

Always trace the map to the final consumer – however remote they may seem

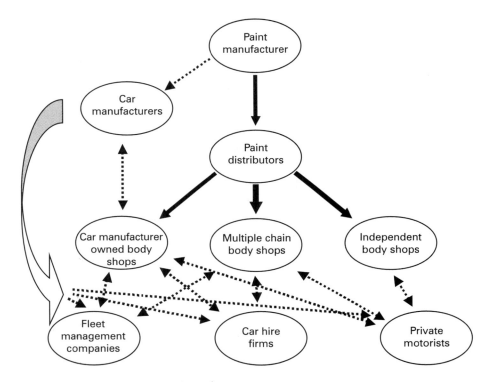

Figure 4.3 Market map including the consumer

clear sales link to these end-users, and it also has a desire to pull these users back through its own body shops when it comes to servicing and repairs. Fleet managers or car hire firms may, on the other hand, like to forge their own links for service contracts and accident repairs.

The importance of the car manufacturer as a key account increases for the paint supplier, but so does the possibility of regarding the likes of an Avis or a PHH (fleet management company) as a key account. Indeed, if the paint supplier can help secure the link between the end-user and the car manufacturer's body shops or a multiple chain, then they have the prospect of a 'double whammy'. The pressing question becomes, which 'double whammy' to go for?

But the map is still not complete, and Figure 4.4 adds yet another key influencer: the insurance company.

The insurance company has a key say on where the driver should go to have the car repaired and can therefore have a significant influence on the paint manufacturer's future. Not surprisingly the insurance company now is added to the ranks of potential key accounts.

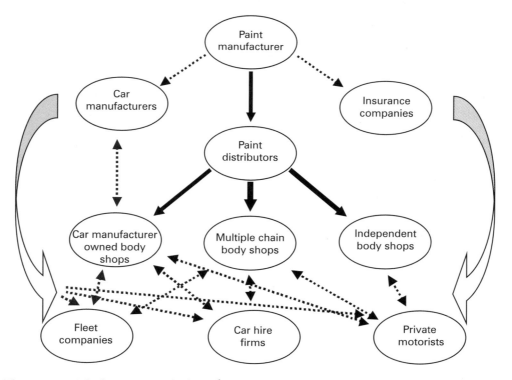

Figure 4.4   Market map including the insurance company

Note that when building up this map the potential key accounts do not have to be direct customers of the supplier – *key influencers* should also be considered as candidates for the title, though some may prefer to distinguish them by using the label *key influencer* rather than *key account*.

'The battle of the first call'

There is still much to add to this map, but let's draw a line here and consider an important dynamic of this particular marketplace – we might call it the 'battle of the first call'.

You have just scraped your car. Where do you go first for help – the body shop, the insurance company, the manufacturer? Clearly where you go could have a hugely important impact on where you end up, and so what paint is finally applied. The paint manufacturer must take an interest in this battle. More than that, if it wants to be an influential player in this market, it must also aim to influence the routing of that call.

If the call goes through the insurance company, then perhaps the paint manufacturer can influence the insurance company to push you towards a body shop that uses its paint. This might be a relatively easy task of persuasion, but the loyalty of the insurance company to a particular make of paint is likely to be low. This route is, then, easy to influence, but hard to 'lock in'.

Perhaps the paint manufacturer tries to tie you more directly with the car manufacturer's body shops. This might be done through the technology of the paint application, the precision of the colour matching, or even by some use of the e-revolution.

Imagine that, having just bumped your car, your mobile phone sends out the equivalent of a distress call, but not to the emergency services, to the nearest available body shops. Back comes a call with instructions of how to get there, perhaps even through the on-board GPS navigation system.

Far-fetched or not, what is clear is that influencing the end-user through this route will be much harder. But if it could be done, and it was the paint supplier that helped to forge the link, then imagine the level of loyalty built up between the paint and car manufacturers. Hard to influence, but great for 'lock in'.

Opportunity chains

This is a typical example of the sort of choice facing a supplier in this kind of market; which route to take – the easy to influence but promiscuous one, or the hard to achieve but high loyalty option? Or can both be chased in parallel, perhaps by forging links between the car manufacturer and the insurance company?

The more you know, the greater the choice, and the better the decision

Once we map out the total market we can start to see what we will call 'opportunity chains' – particular routes of influence and revenue that we may choose to target and exploit. The chain should always be followed through to the end-user, for it is very often at this end of the chain that the greatest opportunities occur.

Where are the key accounts now?

Who then are the key accounts in all of this? The question is really: Which opportunity chain, or chains, provide the best future for us? The distributor, historically the obvious choice, has receded somewhat into the background once the full market map is analysed. The body shops themselves are similarly of less importance than might have been supposed. Now try this for a scenario.

The key accounts are selected from the car manufacturers and the insurance companies, with the intention of forming links between them. This is clearly a complex task and will call on the diamond style of relationships described in Step 2. But there is still the task of making sure the product is placed in the body shops, and that is a task for a hunter sales team operating to the bow-tie model (also described in Step 2). Key account management doesn't necessarily replace or kill previous means of doing business, but it can effect significant changes on the purpose and application of those means.

Application exercise

Take some time with the team to draw out the most comprehensive and all-inclusive map of your market that you can manage. The more you know, and the more you include, the more complex the final diagram will be, but the more instructive the exercise.

Some tips:

● Take the map right through to the end-consumer, even if you have no direct contact with them.

- Include influencers on the purchase decisions even if they are not direct customers, or even if they don't actually buy any product at all. A key account does not have to be a 'debtor'. (I recall one finance director being very certain when asked who the company's key accounts were, replying: 'Our largest debtors').

- Draw on lines to represent the movement of product or the sale of services – *the revenue lines*.

- Mark on the map the size of the revenue (or profit, if you can) at each point. It will be useful to show the total market figure and then your own share as a comparison – a great way to highlight your strengths, and to indicate opportunities.

- Draw on lines to indicate where demand is established and where influence is applied – *the influence lines* (expect this to get complex and messy!).

- When considering influence, don't forget the e-revolution. Lines of communication between players in the market have been opened up dramatically by the Internet and by e-mail, let alone the more complex modes of e-commerce. Today, almost anybody can talk to anybody, if both parties think there may be something in it.

- Using these lines of revenue and influence, identify the main *opportunity chains*.

- Mark on the map where you currently have contacts and involvement in these chains. Indicate where those contacts are good and sufficient and where they are perhaps poor and insufficient.

- Without drawing firm conclusions as yet, look at where you have traditionally seen your key accounts and ask yourself if that still holds true.

- You probably started by putting yourself at the top of the diagram. This tends to force a certain view of the market. For freshness and variation, try putting yourself in the centre – sometimes it just works.

Step 5

The marketing plan and market segmentation

Your business has a business plan, and it also has a marketing plan, perhaps more than one as it will have a marketing plan for each market you operate in, and maybe you also have segment plans as subsets of those marketing plans.

OK, let's be honest – *is* this the case, or are we in the land of make believe here?

Let's just suppose it *is* the case, the next questions are: Are those marketing plans and segment plans up to date? Are they shared across the business? And are they implemented?

Too many (perhaps most) marketing plans are based on data from more than three years ago, are stamped 'company secret' and so are accessible only by the 'gilded ones', and slowly gather dust on top shelves. (If you have no marketing plan, or any of these problems are true for you, then you might like to turn for help to the reading list in Next Steps... at the end of this book.)

Now, if of course none of these criticisms applies to you, and you really do have well-documented market and segment plans, then you have a massive head start on identifying your key accounts. So much so that what we are calling Step 5 in this process would have already been done in your case, right back at the start. Your business plan would have determined the objectives of your marketing plans, which in turn cascade down into your segment plans, and your key accounts lie within your segment plans. Figure 5.1 shows the normal hierarchy in the planning process.

For you then, Step 5 is more of a review, to check that your thinking on key accounts is in line with your approach to market segmentation. If, however, you have some doubts about the thoroughness of your segmentation, Step 5 will be an opportunity to reassess and to think afresh.

Markets first, segments second, then identify your key accounts

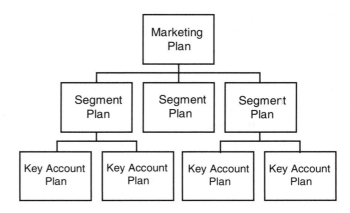

Figure 5.1 The normal hierarchy in the planning process

If your task is bigger than review or reassessment, perhaps as big as establishing your segmentation strategy from scratch, then you will certainly want to look beyond the bounds of this book (see Next Steps… for some guidance on this).

It is worth taking a moment to review what is meant by segmentation, what it does for a business, and its huge importance in the selection of key accounts.

THE MARKET SEGMENT

A market segment is a grouping of customers with similar buying needs, attitudes and behaviours.

It is important to stress the last two words, 'attitudes' and 'behaviours'. If we only looked at needs, we would be severely limiting our options. We all *need* food, and if that was our only consideration there would be only one segment in the food market – food! Of course there are dozens of segments because beyond mere need we display an amazing array of attitudes to the stuff, and exhibit an equally large range of ways of going about buying and using it. Each of these facets of behaviour or attitude provides a potential market segment. Just consider a few of those in the food market:

- eating out – restaurants, cafés, fast food, food on the move, vending…;
- eating in – breakfast, lunch, dinner, entertaining, barbecues…;
- business – canteens, hotels, institutions, catering, airlines…;

- retail – supermarkets, wholesalers, cash and carry, delicatessens...;
- branding – brands, own brand, no brands...;
- health – low sodium, diet, low fat, high fibre...;
- diet – vegetarian, vegan, organic...;
- ethnic – Indian, Chinese, Italian, Moroccan...;
- family – 2.4 kids, single parent, retired, single...;
- experience – cordon bleu, first-time cooks, professionals...;

Add to this list the range of food fads, local tastes, traditions, income levels, time to cook, lifestyles and more, and you can see that the list is huge. So huge that we need to find ways to aggregate some of these micro-segments, to find what we will call 'viable' segments.

The 'viable' segment

A viable segment should stand up to these questions:

- Is it large enough to justify focused attention?
- Are the customer's needs, attitudes and behaviours similar enough to be aggregated together?
- Are the needs attitudes and behaviours specific enough to be distinguishable from other segments?
- Is it possible to design an appropriate *marketing mix* for the segment? (See below.)
- Is the segment *reachable;* can it be identified, measured, analysed, communicated to, and sold to, *discreetly* from other segments?

SEGMENTATION AND THE MARKETING MIX

Segmentation is a three-step process:

1. Deciding on what basis to 'slice' the market into segments.
2. Choosing those segments that you wish to be active in.
3. Targeting each of those active segments with a unique *marketing mix*.

The supplier aims to influence demand and gain competitive advantage through the application of the marketing mix, often known as the four 'P's – product, price, promotion, and place, shown in Figure 5.2.

By preparing a different and specific marketing mix for each segment, the business ensures that it will meet the needs of each grouping of customers in a more focused way. Such a focus will help ensure competitive advantage, and so greater profitability.

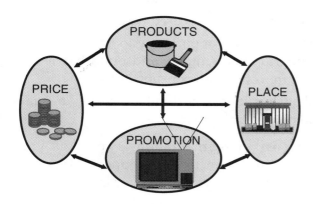

The marketing mix

Figure 5.2 The marketing mix

BENEFITS OF SEGMENTATION

There are many benefits to be had from good segmentation:

- An enhanced understanding of the market dynamics, particularly the notion of the *opportunity chains* (see Step 4) that run right through to the end-consumer.
- An enhanced understanding of competitor strengths (the competition will differ by segment), and so the opportunities for competitive advantage.
- Greater understanding of the needs, attitudes and behaviours of customers.
- A better chance that you will see how to develop the capabilities of your business in order to match those needs.
- A basis for organizing and structuring your business – focusing the whole supply chain on the customer.
- Improving your ability to manage the marketing mix, in a customer-focused way.
- Enhancing your opportunity to add value, gain competitive advantage, and build barriers to entry for competitors or substitutes.
- Enhancing your opportunity to create, maintain and defend price premiums.

The purpose of segmentation is to focus your limited resources on to those opportunities that will take you where you wish your business to be, and represent the best chance for you to gain competitive advantage.

Failure to segment will at best result in missed opportunities, and at worst, in the inability of your business to gain competitive advantage and long-term security.

SEGMENTATION AND KEY ACCOUNTS

It will be clear by now that segmentation and KAM go hand in hand. They have similar aims – the focus of limited resources on to the best opportunities. And they present similar challenges – not least the need to make choices.

Without segmentation the selection of key accounts will tend to suffer from 'sizeism'. Step 6 will introduce a tool that helps us identify key accounts on the basis of their attractiveness to us and our strengths with them. The tool requires that we can make comparisons between different customers on this basis. Without segmentation, most markets are too large and diverse for this to be workable – what seems attractive in one part of the market is not so important in another – and so the scale of business becomes the only truly comparable factor – hence 'sizeism'. The 20 per cent of customers that supply 80 per cent of the business will be the key accounts.

Why segmentation must come first

This is how some businesses end up devoting huge sales efforts to 'big' customers that operate in segments of little future interest, while the marketing staff grow ever more frustrated that attention is not being given to the 'small' customers in those segments identified as being vital to the business future. When the team is assembled at Step 3, bear this particular point in mind and ensure that both sales and marketing are properly represented.

It can be worse than this of course. If there is no proper segmentation in the first place, then the 'big' customers will simply become the basis of your segmentation – where they go, then there must you. Fine if you get lucky and they take you somewhere good; not so fine if they are chasing their own interests with no regard to yours.

Every customer their own segment

In theory a segment could be as small as an individual customer, with their own unique needs, attitudes and behaviours. In practice this may indeed become possible through KAM. Whether this is so or not will depend greatly on the type of industry and market.

In fast-moving consumer goods (FMCG) markets, while the e-revolution and concepts such as customer relationship management (CRM) suggest the prospect of every *consumer* their own segment, in practice it is still very helpful (and practical) to aggregate customers together under some general definitions. In some B2B (business-to-business) markets it may indeed be possible to view a *customer* as a segment, provided that there are not so many customers that the supplier will be pulled apart at the seams.

We have seen from our brief description of what KAM might involve (Step 3), that whatever else, it certainly involves effort. The channelling of resources, and particularly people, is perhaps its most distinctive feature. If every customer is regarded as absolutely unique, then there are two difficulties: either only a very few can receive such attention (a *very* few), or resources will be spread so thinly as to be ineffectual. Segmentation can provide the solution to this dilemma, by identifying and clustering customers with such similarity of needs, attitudes and behaviours that what suits one will surely suit another. A benefit of KAM in such a circumstance is the way that working with what we might call a 'lead key account' will benefit our efforts with other accounts (key or otherwise) clustered in that segment.

Helping us select our key accounts

For our purpose in this book, the selection of key accounts, we can see one very particular benefit of segmentation – it will simply make the task easier.

In Step 4 we considered the car refinish market as an example of market mapping. Let's take another type of paint, household decorative paint, to illustrate this particular benefit of segmentation.

ICI Dulux in the UK supply paint to DIY users through the retail channels, and to the professional decorators through distributors and some direct supply. DIY and professional decorators represent two distinct segments of the decorative paint market. Within those segments there are many further segments or subsegments, but for the sake of the example we will leave the 'cut' at this level.

'Big' sometimes *is* beautiful – it depends on the nature of the market segment

If we now just take one factor that might determine customer attractiveness, we will immediately see the importance of segmentation in key account selection. Let's consider scale. (Yes, I know I have knocked scale a dozen times, but it *is* a factor, just not the *only* one.)

In the DIY market, the goal of brand leadership makes the large DIY superstores very attractive customers. They take Dulux everywhere they go, and these days that's most places. Big does indeed mean good for a business seeking national coverage and brand leadership. Add to this the fact that national retailers need strong national brands and the case is strengthened.

In the professional decorator market, a large firm means large-scale contracts, which means pressure on price often without the same counter-argument of a strong consumer brand franchise. Not so attractive. The real key accounts lie elsewhere, perhaps the distributors, perhaps the specifiers, perhaps the architects.

HOW TO SEGMENT THE MARKET

For a full and proper treatment of this particular challenge you might turn to *Key Marketing Skills* by Peter Cheverton (Kogan Page, 2000). For our purposes here a brief summary will suffice.

The good news is that we have already started the process. Step 4 was about drawing up a market map, and that is the first step to segmenting the market – a full picture. Onto this full picture we started to put *opportunity chains*, particular routes to market and to end-consumers that presented us with options and, indeed, opportunities.

Next we must look to see at what points in these chains we might choose to make our 'slices'. We might look for what we will call 'leverage points'. These are points in the chain where critical purchasing decisions are made, or significant influences are applied. In looking for these points don't just look for where the decision to buy is made, also look for where the decision *not to buy* may be made or influenced.

At this stage there are some important factors to consider, among them:

- Are decisions made globally, regionally, or locally?

- Do retailers and distributors make the choice to present your products to the market, or do they simply service demand? In other words, are your products and services 'pushed' into the market by sales effort or aggressive pricing, or are they 'pulled' through by end-user demand?

- Is it the channel that makes the important choices, or the end-user?

- Where does the competition apply its greatest efforts?

- Who buys, what, how, when, and where? Remember a simple truth – markets don't buy anything – it's people who buy every time!

- What are the key attitudes and behaviours – is this a money decision, a performance decision, an image decision?

A fertilizer manufacturer found its product to be in slow decline in a mature market. Competition was increasing, customers were consolidating, and profits were falling. Customer consolidation was a particular worry because as the customers grew larger through consolidation, so they became more important. Their most 'important' customers were fast becoming their least profitable!

The company decided to segment as a means to finding new offers, testing first the more obvious 'cuts' or 'slices': crop type, geography, seasonality, etc. Finally it hit on the simple truth noted above – wheat didn't buy fertilizer, and neither did East Anglia, it was farmers every time!

Farmers came from different backgrounds, with widely differing attitudes, aspirations and buying behaviours. Once the manufacturer started to explore these factors it began to understand (almost for the first time) what *really* made people buy its product, or not. The final segmentation was done on the basis of attitudes and needs, the traditional family farmer, for instance, having a rather different outlook to the graduate of an agricultural college managing a large estate. Division of the

The tale of the fertilizer company – or how segmentation can revolutionize mature business

With thanks to Professor Malcolm Macdonald

Figure 5.3 The fertilizer market divided into seven segments

market into seven segments (shown in Figure 5.3) allowed the business to prioritize its attentions on those that would respond best to its own strengths.

The key accounts were no longer simply the 'big ones', but those customers in each segment that were most attractive, and attractiveness increasingly meant those that 'will respond best to our highly tailored offer'. The resultant marketing mixes helped the manufacturer target its product better, add more relevant value, structure its own operations to suit customers' needs, and gain a significant increase in revenues and profits.

The 'adopters' curve'

This particular method of segmentation has a lot of attractions to those interested in identifying key accounts, because the same criteria can be used to identify both the target segment and the target key account.

When a new product is launched there is usually a vanguard of ardent enthusiasts that jump on board, sometimes almost regardless of the product's merits. Often it goes no further and the product dies, remembered only as a fad supported by a clique of fanatics.

If a product is to succeed, it has to go beyond that narrow following and find a wider audience. It has to progress beyond the *innovators* to find the *early adopters*. Everett Rogers captured this concept in his much quoted 'adopters' curve' shown in Figure 5.4 (see page 62). The curve shows how most new products or ideas go through stages of adoption, first by the innovators, a small but enthusiastic group, then by the early adopters who help make the product something of wider appeal. The early majority provide the volume sales that drive down costs and turn the product into a mass-market one such that the late majority come sweeping in to buy. Laggards are those that resist till the very end, or perhaps never succumb.

A classic example of such a development is the electronic pocket calculator. The first calculators were cumbersome instruments, often with a mind-boggling array of functions from cosines to recip-rocals. They were bought as an advanced scientific instrument, predominantly by businesses and insti-tutions, with purchase doubtless requiring approval by the capital acquisitions committee. It was not long, however, before a new segment of the market opened up, spurred on by government legislation. Once it was approved that calculators could be used

How we 'adopted' the pocket calculator

The 'adopters' curve'

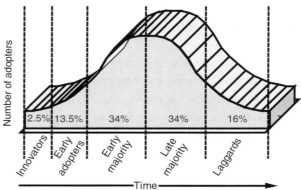

With acknowledgements to Everett Rodgers

Figure 5.4 The 'adopters' curve'

in 'O' level maths exams children rushed home to demand that their parents bought them one. This new demand from the early adopters brought prices tumbling down. Before long the pocket calculator was an established item for business people and this early majority helped drive prices even lower until calculators were being given away free as promotional items; the late majority was engaged.

An interesting feature of the model is the role of the innovator, sometimes a positive force, but not infrequently a drag on the market's uptake. The Internet is a case in point. Early users of the Internet were portrayed as 'nerds', sad characters with no social life who sat up late at night surfing the Net in search of other such lost souls. Whether true or not, this image of the early users served to hold back wider acceptance of the Internet, perhaps for as long as two years.

As a model for segmentation, the adopters' curve holds much promise, and also as a method of identifying key accounts. If your offer is new, leading edge, challenging, even risky, then you will need to find your key accounts among the innovators and the early adopters of the market. If your offer is well established, secure, safe, perhaps even a little staid, then it will be to the other end of the curve that you may need to look.

Be wary, however, of the innovators who may be easy to sell to but will suck up your resources and may prove fickle and promiscuous when the next new thing comes along. Early adopters and early majority types may be your most secure targets in the long run.

Application exercise

Depending on how well established your current segmentation of the market is already, you have either a relatively easy or a major task on your hands.

Assuming it is in good order, review the objectives set for KAM, the resources you have at hand and how you plan to use them, and make sure that these are in line with the objectives of your marketing and segment plans.

Assuming it to be there, but ripe for improvement, use your work at Step 4, the market map, to look for new approaches. Take particular note of the more attractive opportunity chains.

And if you have no segmentation in place, make this a top priority before proceeding any further with your key account selection. Yes, this will slow you up, but getting it right now will save you much regret (and embarrassing back-pedalling) later.

Step 6

The key account identification and selection matrix (KAISM)

Focus on the future, not the past.

There is an absolutely key point to note when selecting your key accounts. It has been made before, but it is a point so important that I make no apologies for repeating it:

It is far too easy for businesses to define their key accounts as today's largest customers.

Easy, and hugely dangerous. If your market environment really is so mature or so static that nothing changes over five or six years, then perhaps you can get away with such a definition – but even then this is a very risky 'perhaps'.

Too many businesses take this rather lazy approach to selection and the result is all too predictable – these 'big customers' decline, and having given them all your best resources, and attention, you have none to spare to chase the newly emerging customers.

Perhaps your largest customers today *were* your key accounts at some time in the past, and maybe that is how they grew to such a size, but times change. The future's biggest customers may be quite small today, perhaps they are not yet even customers of yours, but that doesn't stop them being key accounts.

Give yourself a quick test

List today's biggest customers – the 'top ten'. Then list the 'top ten' from five years ago, and from ten years ago. Compare the lists. If the list has changed dramatically, imagine how much it will change again in the next five and ten years, given that the pace of change is ever increasing.

If the lists are very much the same, dare you assume that the next five years will be as uneventful? A feature of many mature markets where businesses have ceased growing by double-digit percentages is that they have become cash rich but with nowhere in particular to go. This is a favourite scenario for the takeover bid, and a short burst of buy-outs and sell-offs can transform your customer list overnight.

Jam today or tomorrow?

We need a better means of selecting our key accounts than studying our recent sales history. But at the same time, can we honestly conceive of calling our largest customer anything but a key account?

Here we encounter an all too common dilemma – how to focus on the future health of the business when our bosses and our shareholders demand performance today. To understand how far your key accounts will contribute to current or future performance, remind yourself of the definition of a key account suggested at the beginning of Step 1 – in short, a key account is an investment in the future. To elaborate:

A key account is a customer in which we are prepared to invest a significant share of our company's resources (time, people, money) in the belief that that customer represents the best route to achieving our long-term business ambitions.

Imagine yourself a gardener, and your key account to be a choice specimen that you have just taken from the seed tray to plant out. Having prepared the soil, planted it out, fed it and watered it in, would you go back in a week's time and wrench it out to see if any roots have grown? Of course not, instead you will return each week to nurture the plant, in the belief that your attentions are worth it and that a prize-winning plant will result. The same goes for key accounts.

Don't 'kill' your key account investments by overly short-term expectations

Your key accounts are there for the long haul – so what of the jam required today? Well, there are your biggest customers, and there are the ones that you have most success with right now, and the ones that chase you and you happily respond to even though you know them to be your past, not your future. Perhaps somewhere in there we can find some jam for today?

Who chooses whom?

Simply calling a customer a key account will achieve nothing. For one thing your entire organization must recognize them as such and behave accordingly. And if you think that's a big challenge, how about this one – the customer has to let you treat them as a key account or else the venture will end in expensive frustration.

Naming them 'key' is one thing...

You can't force a relationship on customers – they will allow you in just as far as they see there being benefit to themselves – and if they do not see you as a worthy suitor, then don't expect that to be very far at all. In short, if you have no competitive advantage you cannot expect much return from the exercise of KAM. Here we have another dilemma for we are of course in the world of 'the chicken and the egg' – the purpose of KAM is to find the route to competitive advantage, yet the opportunity to practice it without any such advantage is significantly limited.

... the practice of KAM requires a mutuality of 'high regard' – are you a key supplier?

THE KAISM EXPLAINED

The purpose of the key account identification and selection matrix KAISM (see Figure 6.1) is to provide a process for handling these two dilemmas – 'Jam today or tomorrow?' and 'Who chooses whom?' – as well as a host of other issues.

The matrix plots customers (current *and* potential) as a result of considering two sets of factors. These sets of factors represent the two sides of a mutual selection process: yours (do you like them?), and theirs (do they like you?). Customer attractiveness is what it is that makes customers, or potential

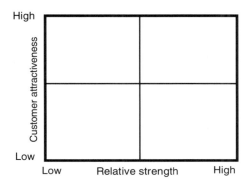

Figure 6.1   The 'KAISM' key account identification and selection matrix

The 'KAISM' key account
identification and selection
matrix

customers, attractive to you. Relative strengths are what it is that makes you attractive to your customers in comparison to your competitors.

Each axis will be composed of a range of individual factors, quantitative and qualitative, unique to your own business situation. The importance of defining these factors, and then using them as measures cannot be overstated. If the matrix is to be any kind of guide to allocating resources, deciding priorities, or determining customer relationships, then a great deal of thought should go into this exercise.

Steps 7 and 8 take you through the process of identifying criteria for each axis and rating your customers and yourself against these criteria, a process that will lead you towards the identification of your customers by four broad categories, as shown in Figure 6.2 (see page 70):

- key accounts;
- key development accounts;
- maintenance accounts;
- opportunistic accounts.

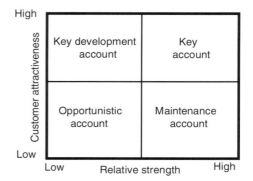

Figure 6.2 Customer categories

A health warning

The KAISM is intended to assist the the brain – not to replace it

Let me stress at this point that while the KAISM provides a process for handling the kind of dilemmas introduced earlier in this chapter, it does not provide hard and fast answers. The moment that the brain disengages and the mathematics of rating and weighting takes over is the moment you are in trouble. If common sense and pragmatism is allowed to give way to the tyranny of a management model, then you will regret the exercise.

The KAISM does not tell you who your key accounts are – it is in fact a far more important tool than that.

PURPOSE AND BENEFITS OF THE KAISM

- To *indicate* where your key accounts *may* lie – you may choose to differ.
- To provoke debate on the criteria for identifying key accounts.

- To identify selection criteria that relate to your long-term business ambitions.
- To gain a business-wide agreement on those criteria.
- To identify potential customers as well as to 'categorize' existing ones.
- To understand the customers' perceptions of your competitive strength.
- To identify what research is required into the customers' needs and perceptions.
- To identify what research is required into competitor strengths.
- To gain business-wide support for those categorized as key accounts.
- To provoke a debate on how to manage and service the other categories of customer.
- To provide a methodology that allows for regular and simple review and updating.

Make sure that you use the KAISM to do *all* these things for you

Process rather than outcome

The final outcome showing customers plotted on the matrix is of much less significance than the debate and the process that puts them there. This is where the team that you gathered at Step 3 will come into its own, providing the means for an intelligent debate, an enhanced understanding, and an outcome agreed across the business.

You should perhaps be forewarned that there are occasions when the final outcome may be of little or indeed no significance at all – let's consider two opposing cases.

The final positioning of your customers on the matrix does not surprise you. This is a common circumstance, particularly in a mature market where relationships have been managed over some time. You knew in your bones who would end up where. So why bother going to such lengths? The answers are in the purpose and benefits of the KAISM list above.

Perhaps there *is* a surprise in the outcome, and a customer that has been regarded as a sure-fire key account (perhaps already managed as such) appears somewhere else on the matrix. It is unlikely that such a customer would be removed from the list as a result of this exercise, but a debate is provoked, understanding is improved, perhaps criteria are reconsidered, and maybe the customer finds its way back into the top-right quadrant. So again the question: What was the point of such efforts if you were not going to accept the outcome? Once again the answers are in the list shown above.

Debate the outcome, don't just believe it

Surprises in the top-left quadrant?

The exercise is of increasing value the newer you are to the market, either as a business or as a team of individuals. If you have long since penetrated as far as you can go, then there will be few surprises in the top-left quadrant, but in a new venture, or in a rapidly expanding market, expect to see perhaps the majority of customer names in this top-left space. These names should include, of course, all those that are not yet customers, but you clearly wish to win.

Once you've done this exercise, don't consign it to a dusty upper shelf. The beauty of the KAISM process is that it is very easy to review and to update

– the hard work comes with the initial creation. This makes it an ideal tool for reviewing your definitions, *at least* on an annual basis if not more frequently.

MANAGING THE FOUR CATEGORIES – AN INVESTMENT PORTFOLIO

It is not within the scope of this book to provide guidance on the management of key accounts (*Key Account Management: A complete action kit of tools and techniques for achieving profitable key supplier status*, 2nd edition, by Peter Cheverton, published by Kogan Page, 2001, devotes itself to this issue), or indeed the other categories of customer, but it is important to stress that the success of any KAM strategy depends on having a plan for *all* categories of customer.

The identification of customers by these four categories does not imply the abandonment of some for the sake of the others. Nor does it recommend an elitist approach that can see the development of a dangerous 'in and out' view of customers and a damaging 'them and us' divide in the sales team. It is primarily a means for determining the allocation of resources. That a key account will get more resources than a maintenance account does not necessarily make it more important, simply different.

Figure 6.3 (see page 74) indicates the way that the allocation of resources must be viewed, investing those most valuable of all resources, people and people's time, in the key accounts and the key development accounts. Other less resource-demanding means of managing and servicing the maintenance and the opportunistic accounts must be found. If

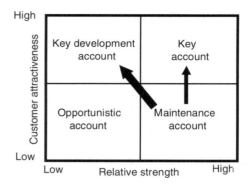

Freeing up the energy to invest in key accounts

Figure 6.3   Freeing up the energy to invest in key accounts

this is achieved, then not only can the time and energy saved be invested in customers in the upper half of the KAISM, but so can the improved profits that will be harvested as a result of the more efficient management of those in the lower half.

One of the apparent ironies of KAM is that your key accounts may not always be the most profitable customers *today*. If we remember our definition of a key account – an investment in the future – then we will see why this is in fact not the irony it seems, but a natural outcome of investment and harvest decisions.

Measuring profitability

This brings me to an all-important point, the need to measure customer profitability – by customer. How can you make any of the decisions to allocate resources if you don't know what impact that will have on profit? Putting more effort into key accounts may actually reduce profits in the short term in pursuit of a longer-term increase (if you were able to

The only 'absolute rule' of KAM? Absolutely

measure profitability to the level you should, you would be able to observe this), but remember they are investments. Also, we want to know whether removing resources from some customers improves their profitability.

APPROPRIATE PLANS

Having given the necessary health warnings and understood the real purpose and benefits of the KAISM, we can make a few comments on how to handle the customers put into each category.

The key accounts

You have a mutual regard for each other that justifies the allocation of resources designed to develop the relationship. People and time are the critical ingredients, with a key account team devoted to improving their understanding of the customers' needs and aligning the business to act upon them. These are customers that must be grown and developed if the investment is to be repaid.

People and time...

The key development accounts

It is quite usual for the majority of customer names to be found in this quadrant. This is after all where a customer that you are chasing but have not yet won would be positioned, and most businesses have more customers to win than to keep.

The principal tasks will be exploratory – researching needs and perceptions, and gaining entry. This is a classic case of 'the chicken or the egg'

... exploration

– how to gain entry with no understanding of needs, how to understand needs with no adequate contacts.

These customers will also be very demanding on resources, with a relatively slow payback from the investment. Remember, you have limited resources, don't spread them too thinly. How many key development accounts could your business chase, simultaneously?

There will almost inevitably be a difficult selection task with customers in this quadrant. If you do indeed have a large number of key development accounts, it may be worth repeating the whole KAISM exercise just for this group, in order to high-light the very attractive and to identify those with the most prospect of progress. There remain plenty of options for your approach here. You could increase your resources if the opportunity was very attractive, or you could 'pick them off' as specific customer opportunities arise. In this quadrant you must be prepared to experiment, to trial, and to allocate resources as 'test cases', aiming to learn from each experience.

... and experimentation

Some businesses appoint their most junior sales-people to look after these customers as a sort of training or proving ground, or attach them to the responsibilities of account managers already burdened by too many 'top right' key accounts. Where this is done because the business doesn't see much real prospect of progress, then they are usually right – they make no progress! Another common approach is to make such customers the responsibility of the telesales team, expecting them to develop relationships that will enhance the customer's view of you, by telephone.

Undeniably there is a need for energy and persistence here and many businesses see these customers as the natural preserve of their best 'hunters' (see Step 2). Some even set up specific hunter teams, often called business development, or new horizons, or some such forward-looking term. This may be appropriate, but in such cases it is often necessary to manage the transition of customer responsibility away from this hunter team to a farmer key account manager and team. This is far from easy – customers often resist such changes, and it will be as well to consider how this transition might be managed before creating such hunter teams.

The maintenance accounts

Above all else these customers must be retained. But in addition to that, they must be managed with an eye to reducing the kind of resources that will be required for key and development accounts.

In many ways this is the hardest category. These are good customers, perhaps they have been loyal for years, almost certainly they are personal favourites of plenty of your team. The tough decision, but the right one, is to pull resources and energy back from such customers – it is needed elsewhere.

Freeing-up energy and resources…

Some people (and very often it is the sales rep responsible for such a customer) might say you were abandoning them. Sales people don't like the idea of 'dropping' customers, after all the work that has gone into winning them, and who can blame them? But this category is not about abandonment, it is about finding ways of looking after customers that won't trap you and your team into time-consuming commitments.

Perhaps sales visits can be made less often, supported by an upgraded and well-trained inside sales or telesales team. This isn't easy, and beware the cost-cutting drive to put them on to a call centre. If this is done badly, many customers pushed this way will never bother to avail themselves of your new service. Having said that, call centres can be great, for those that *want* to deal with you that way. Forms of e-commerce might provide the solution in many cases, but take care to implement such systems only if they do indeed work to the customer's benefit, not just yours. Often the customer might even prefer such an arrangement, if it seems more appropriate to his or her needs.

It may be necessary to reduce or remove services – access to technical support, provision of information – or even to charge for its provision. Not easy, but if you are to practise proper KAM, you must find solutions to such problems, and solutions that don't lose you your customers' high regard.

Often, the success or failure of dealing with newly identified maintenance accounts lies in how the transition is handled. Let's say your solution is to take an account, currently supplied directly from your own distribution network, and place it in the care of local distributors. Compare two alternative approaches to such a transition:

... it's as much how you do it as what you do...

Approach 1: Apologies are sent to the customer, including a letter from the MD thanking the customer for their loyal support, and hoping that it will continue, despite the need to reorganize business operations. The distributor is given the account, to work with how it sees fit. Once the handover is decided on, and the necessary meetings have been concluded, the previous sales contact has no further contact with the customer.

Approach 2: The supplier and the distributor make a joint presentation on the advantages to the customer of moving to a local distributor, including shorter lead times, more frequent delivery, flexible terms, product variants to suit local circumstances, and more personal attention. The distributor is helped to understand their new customer by the previous sales contact, who stays in touch over a managed handover period.

Whatever your solution, the task is to free your time, and your team's time, and to sell the changes to your maintenance customers, positively. I have heard one CEO talk about 'aggressive maintenance' – it's not a bad phrase.

The opportunistic accounts

These are customers that you will service willingly as and when it suits your priorities. You should not make wild promises that you cannot keep, nor should you treat them like nuisances. Be pleased of their custom, but recognize it for what it is – income that helps you develop your key accounts and key development accounts.

... as and when you can... good territory for 'hunters'...

Most importantly, don't let such customers steal your resources. Often a juicy order comes along and it's 'all hands to the pumps' to make it happen. Everyone feels good and there are congratulations all round, until it is discovered that in your distracted state you let down a genuine key account. It happens.

SOFTWARE PACKAGES

There are simple systems and complex ones, low cost and high. Be sure to seek advice before taking on any of the higher-cost options. In the end it is best to regard such software as clever calculating tools that will help make your presentation of data look more professional. The real value is still in the brainwork, not the software.

A simple package can be obtained free of charge from INSIGHT (see Next Steps...). The software will remove any need for complex mathematics on your part, and it will provide you with a simple means to record and update your analysis as well as producing a printed output, but the software is no substitute for debate and for the application of brain power.

Application exercise

Selecting the customers for selection
Before moving on to Steps 7 and 8, selecting the criteria for the two axes, there is an important piece of pre-selection to be done if you are to avoid two specific problems.

The first problem is a practical one – unless you have only a handful of customers in your market it will be impossible to fit all your customers on to one matrix. Remember, we are as interested in potential customers just as much as existing ones, and that could run into hundreds!

The second problem is that once you start the process of comparing customers' levels of attractiveness, based on the standard set of criteria established in Step 7, you could well find yourself comparing apples to oranges. Can *all* customers be compared to a single set of criteria? If your business is in one very distinct market segment, then the answer will be yes, but the more segments you operate in the harder it will become.

The solution to the second problem is in many cases the solution to the first. The KAISM is best used as a tool for distinguishing customers within a specific market segment. Step 5 will have taken you through the process of segmenting your market based on the opportunity chain mapped out in Step 4.

Segmentation first

If you *do* wish to compare customers that operate in different segments, perhaps to identify the whole business's global key accounts, then this *can* be done provided that the criteria used are sufficiently broad.

Some tips:

If you are doing this the first time around, then you may be well advised to select a small sample group of customers. Perhaps deliberately selecting names that you expect to fall into each of the boxes, almost as a test of the process. You can then build on that foundation.

Pre-select a sample list

You do not need to compare everyone to everyone – customer groups of up to 10 at a time are both practical and sufficiently indicative.

Do it as a paper exercise first...

The first time round, do it as a paper exercise and don't worry too much about absolute precision. This is what we might call the 'quick and dirty' approach. The value of this is that it gets you started without becoming paralysed by analysis, and that it keeps your brain in gear. Once you switch (if you do) to a software approach there is a danger that arguments over the number of decimal places can overtake you, and worse, the brain is replaced by fingers on keys.

There is also a danger to the 'quick and dirty' approach – that you might leave it there as a finished job. 'Quick and dirty' can often mean, 'what we already knew to be the truth', and such laziness could be very damaging in the long run. If you do this exercise in an hour it will be an hour wasted.

You might choose to assess those customers that you already define as key accounts – to compare them to each other. This can be a useful exercise, but remember that the matrix makes relative comparisons – somebody pretty much always ends up in each box. This being so, don't make the mistake of downgrading genuine key accounts simply because you didn't compare them to non-key accounts!

Repeat the exercise frequently. The more you do it, the less time it will take, and the more accurate it will be. You are never finished with this exercise, there is always more to learn, more to be certain about, and the market changes around you in any case.

And the best tip of the lot – this is a tool, not a master. Let the brain make the tough decisions, and just sometimes even the pit of the stomach can be a helpful guide. Instincts and experience have their place, provided they are recognized as such and not misrepresented as proven facts.

The 'golden rule' of the KAISM

Step 7

Customer attractiveness

To recap, the KAISM (see Figure 6.1) has customer attractiveness on the vertical axis and relative strength on the horizontal. Step 7 is concerned with identifying the factors used to judge customer attractiveness. The range of possible factors is huge, so we had best try to focus our thoughts.

TYPES OF ATTRACTIVENESS FACTOR

There are many types of attractiveness factor, and we might be helped in our search for the right list by approaching them through five different but overlapping considerations. Those that:

- represent 'pure' attractiveness;

- indicate a likelihood of success;
- relate to your long-term business objectives – where do you want to be in x years?
- help to indicate specific opportunities – what can we get?
- are based on a realistic assessment of our resources and capability.

These five considerations are not mutually exclusive, nor must we aim to have one factor from each – the right list cannot be found through such mechanical pigeonholing – but we might hope that our final list will indeed take notice of each of these considerations.

'Pure' attractiveness

Attractiveness factors such as 'large enough to be worth US $1 million profit to us'. On its own, this consideration could be dangerously broad or theoretical – if you like, these are judgements made in a vacuum. Often they serve as givens – nobody smaller than this could be considered attractive, but they don't help us distinguish between two of the same size.

Likelihood of success

These factors aim to indicate how likely it is that those pure attractiveness factors could be made real. They help us to narrow our sights. An example might be that they 'share our view of the future technological solutions'. Of two customers that pass the first 'pure' attractiveness test, perhaps only one passes the likelihood of success test.

Business objectives

If your planned source of competitive advantage is to be some unique added value element in your offer, then you might regard customers that valued that element as attractive. If 'high-tech solutions to customers' problems' is your pitch, then you might expect your most attractive accounts to be those that value such solutions, and are prepared to pay the price for them. If you want to be market leader by volume, then big players may be attractive. If your goal is to be the supplier of highest repute, then that might lead you to a rather different definition of an attractive customer.

Specific opportunities

Let's say you see your future in providing services that are currently provided 'in-house' by most businesses. Your most attractive accounts may be those that have a positive attitude towards outsourcing such services – they provide the most likely opportunity.

Resources and capability

Some customers may be beyond your reach – you're not in the right place, you're not big enough, you're too big, etc. An attractive customer may be one that is easy to gain access to, perhaps because of geography, or existing relationships. These are real-world assessments.

THE PROCESS

Step 7 will take us through the following procedure:

1 Identify a range of possible customer attractiveness criteria.

2 Get it down to six customer attractiveness factors.

3 Weight those factors to indicate level of importance.

4 Rate all customers under consideration against those factors.

5 Multiply the rating by the weighting to identify the relative ranking of customer attractiveness.

6 Position customers along the vertical axis of the KAISM, based on their attractiveness.

Why six factors?

The intention in this step of the process is to identify about six factors that can be applied equally to all customers in the segment under consideration. There are some good reasons not to have too many more or less:

● This tool is one to be used in communicating decisions made about the management and servicing of customers to all throughout the organization – most people will not want to be bothered with huge and detailed lists of criteria – six factors can be remembered.

● The tool is to be used in making some vital, but often hard, decisions – fewer than six factors may be dangerously narrow.

- Another reason has more to do with the process than the outcome. Remember from Step 6 the comment that it was the process that was the more important of these two things. This is going to be a team exercise, and the team will start with a much larger list. 'Getting it down to six' is a good technique for generating debate over what matters.

Of course if you really do have eight, or there really are only four, then go with that.

WORKING THE PROCESS

1. Start by assembling your team, as discussed in Step 3.
2. Ask each member to list his or her own favoured criteria. Ask each person to list at least twelve. You might focus people's minds by asking that at least six should represent their own function's view and at least six the view of the whole business. (This might have been done as pre-work , but never assume that people will do such things; and of course some will overdo it, turning up with the absolute list, no discussion allowed.)
3. An additional 'flavour' can be had if you ask them to list twelve as above, and then another two, three or four, having put themselves into the shoes of another function, and so on for as many different functions as you might like them to consider.
4. Then put your colleagues into pairs or trio groups and ask them to put their lists together so that they have a composite list of at least 20

criteria viewed from all and every angle. They may need to add some more to get to twenty, but don't worry about editing down at this point – that will come soon enough!

5. Now gather together the full team and get all of the possible criteria up on to some flip charts. There will of course be plenty of duplication – to avoid this put one pair's or trio's list up in full and then ask for anything different from the rest of the group.

6. Now, and only now, add any criteria that may already have existed as a result of business strategy discussions or marketing plans (you will need to investigate whether such criteria have ever been set). The reason for doing this now and not at the start is to allow free thinking – no constraints about what 'them upstairs' might have said.

7. Now comes the hard bit – 'getting it down to six'. You may like to call on the help of an impartial (but skilled and knowledgeable) facilitator to get this stage accomplished. There are plenty of perils waiting for whoever stands by the chart with the pen. On the one hand, they will be seen as taking over. The alternative is for them to take part only as the scribe, and that means one valuable view is lost. Most likely of course is that they will take over – the power of the pen. In many ways the worst person to be standing by the chart is the boss, it is far too easy for him or her to impose their view on everyone else.

Suggestions for the task of 'getting it down to six' will be discussed below, but first, and most certainly not to be used to channel anyone's thoughts, the following lists some of the most common criteria put up for consideration of customers:

- Current or short-term sales:
  - measured by volume of sales?
  - measured by value of sales?
  - measured by the profit opportunity?
- Financial stability:
  - Will they be there in the future?
  - Will they pay their bills?

Some typical criteria for assessing customer attractiveness

- Strategic fit:
  - Do they see the world the same way as you?
  - Do they agree on the same approach, the same solutions?
  - Will they take you where you wish to be?
- Cultural fit:
  - Can you get on with them?
  - Will they want to work in the kind of partnership you desire?
- Is future growth potential:
  - measured by volume of sales?
  - measured by value of sales?
  - measured by the profit opportunity?
- Their market standing:
  - Are they an industry leader?
  - Do they have prestige, kudos, or credibility?
  - Will they entice other customers to follow suit?
- Do they adhere to certain ethical, moral, or environmental standards that are important to you?
- Are they early adopters? (See Step 5.)
  - Do they pick up on new ideas and products, or do they wait until the rest of the market has tested them? (If you are offering new

ideas and solutions, then customers with a tendency to buy into new ideas will clearly be attractive.)

- Do they value your offer?
  - Is it relevant to their needs?
  - Will they pay for your expertise or for your 'value'?
  - Do they regard you as a 'value supplier' or as a commodity supplier?
- The level of competition (low being attractive!):
  - Are they winnable?
  - Will competitors fight hard to keep you out?
- Exclusions:
  - Does dealing with one customer prevent you dealing with another? (In markets where confidential information is of extremely high value such as pharmaceuticals, or some FMCG markets, customers may be reluctant to deal with suppliers that deal with their competitors.)
- Closeness of existing relationships:
  - Are relationships good?
  - Do other parts of your business service the customer?
- Ease of access:
  - Are they close geographically?
  - Do they speak your language?
  - Are they open to the kind of relationship you desire?
- Can you make an impact with a realistic resource?

Your own list will doubtless go well beyond these points, your own business circumstances determining what matters to you.

SELECTING SIX FACTORS

How will you get your list down to six factors?

Good old-fashioned debate and discussion will go a long way, but it will also raise some apparently insurmountable sticking points, often between functions whose 'world view' is somewhat different.

Many of the points on the list will be subpoints of others, and a good deal of progress can be made by joining points together, either as extensions or with one point defining the other with extra precision. For instance, if the following two points were on the list:

'They are financially stable' and 'They pay their bills on time'. By joining these we can use one to focus the definition of the other: 'They are financially stable, meaning that they will pay their bills on time'.

Consolidate factors...

Take care, however, with this consolidation technique. In the end, everything can be forced under one heading or another, and some valuable distinctions might be lost.

... but don't lose important distinctions

You might start by deleting the ones that just don't work. There are bound to be some, and a few bold crossings-out can be very good for the team's soul. When you are stuck on a criterion ask whether it would actually help you to choose between two customers. Does it matter enough?

Whenever there is doubt, lean towards those criteria that are most future orientated. Today's revenue matters, but it is not as important as tomorrow's. If today really is more important, then perhaps key account management is not the approach for you right now – perhaps you just need a team of hunters.

Focus on a future orientation

When considering measures of customer performance, particularly financial, your own circumstances will determine whether the volume of sales, the value of sales, or the profit of those sales will be the more important measure. A business seeking to fill its production capacity in order to achieve economies of scale that will be translated into low prices will lean towards measures of volume, while the niche supplier dealing in specialist solutions might prefer a measurement of the profit opportunity.

Some criteria are what we might call 'givens'. Would you seriously consider doing business with anyone who is likely to fold or run off without paying, still less consider them as anything else but opportunistic? Is it helpful then to have such a criteria on your list? The circumstance is all, as you will see when we turn to weighting these factors.

Be wary of too many 'givens'. Selection of the 'vital few' calls for 'differentiators'

Rather than listing givens, for we assume that any customer in our sights comes up to some minimum standards, perhaps we should be listing differentiators – criteria that help us to make clear distinctions between customers.

In your final list, aim to have a mix of factors that takes note of the five considerations listed at the beginning of this chapter. Those that:

- represent 'pure' attractiveness;
- indicate a likelihood of success;
- relate to your long-term business objectives – where do you want to be in x years?
- help to indicate specific opportunities – what can we get?

- are based on a realistic assessment of our resources and capability.

If you really cannot agree on some points, then perhaps you should refer the decision upwards. This is a last resort, and it is hoped that the mere suggestion of such a move is enough to get agreement between you. Of course, if you are the Board, then just pull yourselves together!

Even when you have got a list of six factors, there will doubtless still be debates as to which are more important than others. This need not be a problem for you, as the next but one step in the process – weighting – will deal with this. You will then happily be able to agree that not all factors are equal.

BENCHMARKING

Later in the process you will be giving scores to each customer based on how attractive they are, measured against your attractiveness factors. To ensure consistency in these ratings, you should spend some time deciding what level of attractiveness deserves what rating. For each attractiveness factor set a benchmark of what is good, what is average, and what is poor (greater precision than these three levels is rarely necessary) before starting to rate the customers. For instance, if you have 'the profit opportunity' as a factor, what level of profit reflects good, average, or poor? When rating the customers, you might, for example, give a score between 0 and 3 for those rated as poor, 4–7 for the average, and 8–10 for good.

WEIGHTING

Not all factors are equal

Some things will matter more than others, and giving a weighting to each factor is the way to recognize this. If this seems an unnecessary nicety to you, then that probably indicates that your criteria are pretty even, and that in turn might indicate a fairly stable market environment. Weightings come into their own when times are less stable.

What weightings allow is an indication of the relative importance of factors at a precise moment in time, whether now or at some point in the future. Let's suppose that times are hard and we have some tough targets to meet. At such times we might give a higher weighting to factors that deal with realizable opportunities, and reduce the weighting given to factors dealing with what we called 'pure' attractiveness.

Change the circumstances and we might change the weightings. The market is buoyant and opportunities abound. We can now afford the luxury of pursuing some of those customers that might be harder to win, but will be worth more to us in the long run. Giving higher weightings to factors of pure attractiveness and lower weightings to the factors dealing with realizable opportunities would tend to shift such customers upwards in the matrix.

In the same vein, if your resources are changed – perhaps a number of key sales people leave, or you are allowed to spend extra money on some service provision – then so might your view of attractive customers change. The weightings are the best ways to recognize this. The more abundant your resources, the less important are factors that consider whether customers will demand a 'realistic' share of your resources.

There are two significant benefits to weighting beyond the obvious point of greater precision. First, weighting allows you to work in the real world of juggling long-term objectives with short-term opportunities, and more to the point, get people to understand why you juggle in one direction rather than the other at any moment in time.

Working with a client in Russia, we spent a whole morning identifying a list of six customer attractiveness factors. At lunchtime the manager took me aside and said 'Peter, that was a very valuable process, we have a more common understanding than ever before, but you know, I can't help thinking that right now in Russia only one thing matters – will they pay their bills?'

That afternoon we turned to weightings and financial stability got a 90 per cent share.

Weightings recognize the reality of the circumstances

Secondly, the benefit of changing the weightings to represent these shifts of circumstance is that the factors themselves can 'stay put'. This will be enormously beneficial when you remember that a key purpose of this activity is the communication of 'who and why?' to the whole business. If the customer attractiveness factors keep shifting, then those valuable support functions might just conclude that it's just those salespeople changing the goalposts again.

The weightings should of course add up to 100 per cent. They should be recorded as shown on Table 7.1 on page 98.

RATING, WEIGHTING AND RANKING

Table 7.1 provides us with a means of recording the rating of customers and calculating their relative positions on the vertical axis of the KAISM.

1. Enter your chosen customers across the top of the table.
2. Enter your selected and agreed customer attractiveness factors.
3. Enter the agreed weighting for each factor.
4. Rate each customer against each factor, giving a score from 1 to 10 in each case, placing the score in the top left of each box. The higher the score, the better your customer meets that particular definition of attractiveness. Try to stick to the benchmarks established earlier in the process,

Table 7.1 Ratings and positions of customers on the vertical axis of the KAISM

Attractiveness factor	Weighting %	Customers						
1.	%							
2.	%							
3.	%							
4.	%							
5.	%							
6.	%							
Total weighted score	100%							

The average score:
(Total of all scores divided by number of customers rated)

as it is all too easy to give your 'favourite' customers a better score than they deserve. The benchmark is designed to 'keep you honest'.

It is usually best to work horizontally across the table, ie to choose a factor and rate all customers against that factor, rather than trying to complete the table vertically, rating one customer against all the factors and then moving on to the next one. This will make comparisons more accurate.

5. Again working horizontally across each factor, multiply each rating given (the number in the top left of each box) by the weighting shown for the factor and enter that number in the bottom right of each box. (You may choose to divide all these weighted totals by 100 to avoid too many digits in too small a space!)

It might be at this point that you choose to turn to some computer software for help – the mathematics can start to get quite involved (see Next Steps…).

6. Working vertically now, add all the numbers shown in the bottom right of each box, by customer, and enter a total weighted score for each customer.

7. Calculate the average score. Add all the weighted scores and divide by the number of customers assessed. This average will be used to determine whether a customer is above the line in the KAISM (more attractive than the average) or below the line (less attractive than the average), and how customers sit relative to each other.

Step 8

Relative strengths

In Step 8 you will look at your relative strengths –
how well you stack up, and what you need to know.
This is without doubt the hardest of all the steps,
but done well it is potentially the most valuable. As
with most things in life, effort where it counts pays
dividends. The benefit of this particular process is
that it helps you to see where effort really will count
the most.

Having determined what you think of your
customers in Step 7, you must now complete the
horizontal axis of the KAISM and determine what
your customers think of you.

Some rules:

- Putting yourself firmly in the customer's shoes is
  essential.
- Guessing is not allowed.

- If you don't know, admit it.
- Once you have admitted it, determine how to find out.

Some tips:

- Use the team – you may be surprised who in your organization might have useful feedback on what your customers think of you.
- Ask the customers – you will often be surprised what they will tell you, if you ask, and if you show an interest in the answer.
- Don't let this step of the exercise get you down because of what you don't know. Regard this as something well discovered and use it to determine your market research objectives.

Vendor ratings

Many purchasing organizations work with what they call 'vendor ratings' – sets of criteria for measuring supplier performance. Some companies issue these to their suppliers. Some, like Hewlett-Packard, go as far as issuing league tables to their suppliers. Some companies keep them secret, or at least the buyers do.

Finding out about these ratings is of course invaluable, not just to this exercise, but to your whole business relationship with the customer. Some are very simple – right price, on time in full delivery, and annual rebates – and everyone knows where they are. At least that is what is supposed. In reality most business decisions are taken for reasons more complex than such a simple trio of measures, but they do provide a 'quick and dirty' means of sieving out the good from the bad suppliers. We have of course encountered the 'quick and dirty' approach before, in Step 7, and the buyer is just doing the same in reverse.

Beyond this 'quick and dirty' view, and indeed beyond the buyer's office, lie a whole range of possible measures, some quantifiable but probably mostly rather subjective, that lead to the real heart of the customer's decision-making process.

Other books (see Next Steps…) will help you with your entry strategies, making the right contacts with the members of the customers' DMU (decision making unit), for here we need only note that it is through those contacts that you will find what the customer truly thinks of you.

The bow-tie relationship discussed in Step 2 is far from ideal in such a task. Only one view is represented and buyers will often suggest to you a perception rather different from the whole truth. The old clichés often have a certain truth, 'buyers are people who know the price of everything and the value of nothing'. It is of course the diamond relationship that will bring the full understanding of the customers' needs, their values, and most importantly, their perceptions of you and your competitive standing.

THE PROCESS

Step 8 will take us through the following procedure:

1. Identify a range of possible supplier rating factors used to compare the relative strengths of competing suppliers.

2. Identify the specific and unique set of supplier rating factors used by each customer under consideration.

3. Weight those factors to indicate level of importance.

4. For each factor, rate ourselves against our competitors based on our best understanding of the customers' perceptions.

5. Multiply the rating by the weighting to identify the relative strengths of supplier.

6. Position customers along the horizontal axis of the KAISM, indicating our relative competitive strength with each.

IDENTIFYING SUPPLIER RATING CRITERIA

In much the same way as at Step 7, the team should brainstorm a potential list of criteria that customers might use to assess and to rate suppliers. We will call these the 'supplier rating criteria'.

Clues to what should be on this list can be found in a number of places, including:

- customer vendor ratings;
- customer complaints;
- customer satisfaction surveys;
- requests for tender documents.

There should be criteria representing the five main areas of the customer's concerns:

- financial issues;

- performance issues;
- service issues;
- relationship issues;
- competitive advantage.

The following list has a range of factors that crop up regularly in such exercises:

- Supplier's price.
- Cost in use calculations.
- Total acquisition costs.
- Quality;
  - product effectiveness;
  - product reliability;
  - recalls.
- Value in use;
  - value in the supply chain;
  - cost reduction;
  - reduction of risk;
  - marketing or promotional value;
  - supplier brand names and credibility.
- Level of technical innovation;
  - speed;
  - uniqueness;
  - patents, etc.
- Service levels;
  - on time in full ('OTIF');
  - just in time, etc.
- Speed of response.
- Investment in the industry.
- Long-term sustainability.
- Is the supplier easy to work with? Issues such as
  - 'e' capability;

Some typical factors used to assess suppliers

- dovetailed systems;
- linking supply chains.
- Ability to build partnership relationships.
- Issues of trust and confidence;
  - reliability;
  - track record;
  - ethical standards and behaviour.
- Does the supplier give us competitive advantage?
- Does the supplier work with our competitors?
- The supplier's attitude to exclusivity arrangements.

IDENTIFYING THE CUSTOMER'S UNIQUE SUPPLIER RATING FACTORS

In Step 7 we were looking to consolidate the list of customer attractiveness factors down to six to be applied to all customers. Here in Step 8 we must recognize that every customer has its own unique view, and so its own unique set of supplier rating factors. This is going to be hard work, but worth it.

At this point there are choices. If all the people in this team share an intimate knowledge of particular customers, then it may be a good approach to take some example customers and attempt to narrow the focus on to the factors we believe those customers will use. Perhaps, and it is usually more likely, a small sub-group will have the knowledge required. If so, then this exercise can perhaps best be done away from the general meeting.

It may well be that there is a need at this point to consult with a much wider range of people, including the customer (see below for more on this), in order to uncover the truth, and so the exercise will need to be done in a variety of different ways for different customers.

You may even choose to make use of a professional research agency (see below for more on this).

However it is done, the task is to find a list of factors that we can confidently assert are used by the customer to rate suppliers.

Why this is so important

The importance of doing this task well cannot be overstated. The answers to these questions will determine whether a customer sits to the left or right of the KAISM (see Figure 6.2, page 70). Assuming that they are attractive, this will divide the key accounts (top- right quadrant) from the key development accounts (top-left quadrant). Remember that:

Poor knowledge or wrong assessment will lead to a poor or wrong use of valuable resources

- Key development accounts are much harder work – there are better suppliers than you and some big hurdles to jump.
- Key development accounts will take longer to come good.
- There may be more key development accounts than you can really handle.
- The practice of KAM will be very different in each case, not least in the type and extent of the team deployed (see Step 2).
- Failing to distinguish between key accounts and key development accounts will leave you practising one form of KAM that will inevitably fall between two stools.

If the customer lies in the lower half of the KAISM, then answering these questions will determine whether it is opportunistic or maintenance, and here lies perhaps an even bigger difference in the aims and practice of servicing these two types of customer.

Hitting the right nails

Not only will this task help you to identify your key accounts, but you will be using it to develop greater customer focus across the business and to drive performance improvement programmes. Choosing the right programmes will determine your future success. Setting people off to work on issues that were not really important to the customer can have devastating results for your profitability. Missing out on your areas of weakness, but representing issues that are vitally important to the customer, can have devastating results for your whole business.

Figure 8.1 shows why it is so important to get it right.

Avoid tying up resources in giving unwanted Christmas presents

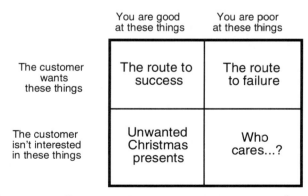

Figure 8.1 Concentrating on areas important to the customer

We all know that success with customers comes from being good at what matters to them, and failure results from being poor at these things, but what about being poor at things that don't matter? Frankly, who cares? And as for being good at things that don't matter, these are just like unwanted Christmas presents, of no perceived value.

Difficulties

I have heard people say that precisely identifying the customers' supplier rating factors cannot be done – the issues are too subjective, they are too varied depending on who you speak to in the customer, and even if you could pin them down, then you are fooling yourself if you think you can truly put yourself in a customer's shoes. And asking customers won't help – there is too much they just will not tell you, let alone the possibility of lies.

Such despair usually comes from two misconceptions about the process. The first is that the process seeks perfect understanding. It does not: it seeks to improve your understanding progressively and continually. This is one of those journeys that we know has no actual arrival point, but that doesn't invalidate the journey. The second misconception is that perceptions don't count because they can't be measured or quantifiably defined. Nothing could be further from the truth, and if hard-to-quantify factors like trust and confidence make it on to the list, then all well and good.

Perfection isn't necessary, or possible

Perceptions matter – try to understand them

Nobody denies that this is a challenge, but it is one worth taking on.

The challenge

Identifying the customer's supplier rating factors will require great honesty. It is tempting to select all those things that you just happen to be good at, and you will doubtless feel very pleased with the outcome, only it will be worthless.

The perceptions of different functions within your own business will be of great value to this debate – each will have its own awareness of what goes down well, and what causes complaints. In addition to this, and I must be careful how I say this, some functions find it easier to take an honest view of customer perceptions than others. Perhaps a certain detachment can sometimes be helpful in seeing the truth – love being blind, and all that?

And yes, to pick up one of the criticisms made of this Step, different people in the customer organization will express different views. This gives you another choice: Do you seek a composite list that represents the customer's view? Might there be value in approaching this exercise from the different functions and departments within the customer, just to understand the variety of requirements? There is huge value in the second option, and do it by all means, but for our narrow purpose of identifying key accounts the first option is the one we will aim for here.

> **Multi-functional teams are hard to work, but they make for more honest self-assessment**

WEIGHTING

In Step 7 we used the weighting of customer attractiveness factors not just to improve precision but to allow us to represent changing circumstances. Perhaps that is also an option here in Step 8.

We have observed that different people in the customer's organization see things differently and their expectations from suppliers may be quite different. If it is possible to arrive at a composite list of factors that represents what we might regard as the total company view, then perhaps we can use the weightings to represent the changing balance between those factors depending on who you are talking to.

When using some of the more sophisticated KAISM software options it is relatively easy to make changes to the weightings if everything else stays the same, and this may help you to see how your competitive strengths relative to other suppliers change depending on the audience.

The weightings should of course add up to 100 per cent and be recorded as shown in Table 8.1 below.

Weightings can be used to reflect the views of different groups within the customer

RATING, WEIGHTING AND RANKING

Table 8.1 provides us with a means of recording the rating of suppliers and calculating their relative positions on the horizontal axis of the KAISM. You will need to complete a separate table for each customer under consideration as follows:

1. Enter the agreed supplier rating factors.
2. Enter the agreed weighting for each factor.
3. For each factor set a benchmark of what is 'good' and what is 'bad' before starting to rate the suppliers. For instance, if you have OTIF (on time in full) as a factor, what will be 'good' – OTIF above 90 per cent? Or is 100 per cent the only standard acceptable, etc.

Table 8.1 Ratings and positions of customers on the horizontal axis of the KAISM

Customer:	Weighting %	Suppliers						
Supplier rating factor		You						
1.	%							
2.	%							
3.	%							
4.	%							
5.	%							
6.	%							
Total weighted score	100%							

The average score:
(Total of all scores divided by number of suppliers rated)

4. Enter the main suppliers along the top.
5. Rate each supplier against each supplier rating factor, giving a score from 1 to 10 in each case, placing the score in the top left of each box. The higher the score, the better the supplier meets that particular requirement. Try to stick to the benchmarks noted in point 3 above, it is all too easy to give yourself better scores than you really deserve, though some people display the opposite tendency and whip themselves throughout this part of the process. The benchmark is designed to 'keep you honest, and keep you balanced'.

It is usually best to work horizontally across the table, ie to choose a factor and rate all suppliers against that factor, rather than trying to complete the table vertically, rating one supplier against all the factors and then moving on to the next. This will make comparisons more accurate.

6. Again, working horizontally across each factor, multiply each rating given (the number in the top left of each box) by the weighting shown for the factor and enter that number in the bottom right of each box. (You may choose to divide all these weighted totals by 100 to avoid too many digits in too small a space!)

   It might be at this point that you choose to turn to some computer software for help – the mathematics can start to get quite involved (see Next Steps…).

7. Working vertically now, add all the numbers shown in the bottom right of each box, by supplier, and enter a total weighted score for each supplier.

8. Calculate the average score. Add all the weighted scores and divide by the number of suppliers assessed. This average will be used to determine whether a supplier is to the right of the line in the KAISM (stronger than the average) or left of the line (weaker than the average), and how the suppliers sit relative to each other.

9. An alternative to point 8 is simply to place the strongest supplier right of the line and rank the rest to the left of the line.

The choice between methods in points 8 and 9 will depend on whether multiple supplier arrangements are common or not in your market. If they are, then the method in point 8 will perhaps be preferred; if there tends, however, to be one dominant supplier, then the method in point 9 may be better.

FINDING OUT WHAT YOU DON'T KNOW

In completing this step of this process you will gain a very clear picture of what you just don't know. There is a high probability that you will have left more question marks on the table than answers. Indeed, it is no bad thing to mark your guesses on the tables (for there will be many if you are honest, even though, strictly speaking, they are not allowed), in order to see your 'ignorance' graphically displayed.

Knowing what you don't know is a huge step forward...

And you can be certain of one thing, there will be a lot of 'ignorance' displayed. In the first place it is very hard to be sure of the supplier rating factors. Given that uncertainty, the business of weighting them is even harder. Then comes the rating. Are you sure you know how the customer *feels*? Remember two things – what they tell you might not be the whole truth, and what they perceive is far more important than what they can measure. And on top of that you then have to rate your competitors. Amazingly, many people get to this point and realize that they do not even know who those competitors are!

Target your research

... provided you do something about it

Use this knowledge of what you don't know to target your research. Perhaps the best research is that conducted by the people who have contact with the customer. Once the key account team is aware of what they don't know, and what they need to know, then they can go about filling the gaps. This is of course yet another 'chicken or egg' question – the gaps in your understanding are probably a result of insufficient contacts, but you have to start somewhere.

Independent research

Given the propensity for most of us either to pat ourselves on the back undeservedly, or to whip ourselves unreasonably, it may be valuable to gain some kind of independent insight as a route to the truth in these matters. Consider formal and independent market research into customer's views, needs, and levels of satisfaction. There are many companies with tools for identifying and measuring customer requirements and customer satisfaction, from surveys to interviews, and beyond. Making use of such expertise may well prove to be one of those early investments that pays handsome dividends in the long run.

And here's another tip – using research as a way of talking to customers will be a good antidote to one of many a supplier's greatest failings – talking too much to themselves.

Asking the customer

If they'll tell you, then why not? Care needs to be taken, however, to ensure that all your questions don't result in one of two bad outcomes.

First, they may determine that you clearly know nothing about them and must be a lost cause. Second, your questions, and more particularly their answers, may build an expectation that something is about to happen. If nothing is about to happen, then frustration can quickly build on the customer's side.

Avoid this scenario at all costs. It would really have been better not to know what the customer wanted in the first place than to ask, be told, and still do nothing about it.

Customers tend to tell least to salespeople they might regard as rather self-interested, and most to those people who they see as having come to help them, such as technical service. Use that truth to determine who in your own team can best find out what is required.

FINAL TIPS

- The process is more important than the outcome.
- Involve the team, don't attempt this alone.
- Avoid disputes over calculations to two decimal places.
- Use the process to determine what you still have to find out.
- Use the process to determine what actions are required to improve performance.
- Repeat the exercise frequently – use it as a review, and aim to improve your accuracy on each reiteration.
- Involve the customer, but avoid building false expectations.

COMPLETING THE MATRIX

Using the information from Table 7.1 (page 98) you will be able to place customers 'north or south' on the matrix – the customer attractiveness axis – and using the information from Table 8.1 (page 112) you will be able to place them 'east to west' – your relative strength with them.

Step 9

Selection and communication

When making your final selection you should keep a few important things in mind:

- The KAISM is a tool to help you, not a master forcing you down roads that look like trouble.
- Yes of course you can break the rules and the definitions – *provided you can explain why*.
- Go back to your resources – how many key accounts can you really manage *properly*? ('Properly' means *so that it makes a difference*.)
- Selection is one thing, getting every one to agree and to support the actions required is far more important.

SELECTION – PRAGMATISM OR THEORY?

Experience shows, perhaps not surprisingly, that the most successful key account relationships exist where the customer has been most open to the concept. You cannot force a relationship on the customer. Is this saying that you should select those customers where it will be easiest to make progress? This could be the route to unambitious mediocrity.

The more weight you give to attractiveness factors that suggest realistic possibilities, and the less to what we called 'pure' attractiveness (see Step 7), the more your final selection will steer you towards the pragmatic route. Yes, there is the danger of unambitious mediocrity, but this route is also more likely to bring early results and rewards. How much you need these early returns will depend on your own circumstances, the pressures on you from bosses and shareholders, and your own objectives for KAM (see Step 1).

What if the hardest nuts to crack really are the most important customers for your future? It is at such a point that your own judgement must prevail over the mathematics of ratings and weightings. Pragmatism and theory must find a compromise. Perhaps one tip might help you with this hardest of all problems. If you are at the start of your key account management journey, then it will help speed it on its way if you can get a success or two under your belt. Perhaps this is the time to lean towards the pragmatic approach. The more experienced you become in the practice of KAM, the more you will be able to take on the challenge of the 'harder nuts'.

CHALLENGING THE OUTCOME

My own business, INSIGHT Marketing and People Ltd, a training and consultancy firm, regularly conducts and reviews this identification and selection process. For many years our chosen criteria for the two axes always found a particular customer down in the bottom-left box. The reason: the company had its own very substantial in-house training organization, never an attractive proposition for a supplier of training, and a hard act to be compared favourably against. But we all knew that this was a key development account, so were we doing something wrong in our analysis?

Disagreeing with the outcome can be good, if you enter into a constructive debate

The attractiveness factor, 'the customer doesn't have its own training organization', was heavily weighted, and therein lay the problem. The factor focused on the present (and so, in truth, the past) and should of course have been something like – 'the customer will not have its own training organization', at some stated point in the future. We had to remember that times change and if the company should close its in-house training organization, then it would be catapulted into the top of the KAISM. Then came the important discussion – rather than wait until that happens, shouldn't we be treating this customer as a key account now, in preparation, perhaps even to encourage the decision to close their own operation?

After a few years the company *did* begin to wind down its own training operation, and our key account attentions began to pay dividends. For a number of years we had a higher strategic intent about this customer than it had about us, a situation with potential for problems if we didn't take care. We would wonder if this mismatch was a problem, a waste of our precious resources, an irritation to the customer? In the event we avoided the problems, largely because we anticipated them. Sometimes you just have to wait, and plan, and in so doing, manufacture your own luck.

By expressing our disagreement with the first result of the KAISM we helped to improve the process, a much healthier response to throwing it all out as 'so much rubbish'.

SELECTION – A BALANCED PORTFOLIO

Select customers in each box of the KAISM, and lay plans for each category

The final KAISM matrix, shown again in Figure 9.1, is perhaps sometimes something of a simplification, but it is still a useful pointer. Those customers that land in the top-left box are there to be developed. There will perhaps be more than can be coped with, and the approach will be largely exploratory. Recognize the work involved here, and the pressure on resources, and select with the greatest care. Those that land in the top-right box are very often there to be retained – you already have a substantial position. Those customers that land in the bottom-right box are there to be managed for cash.

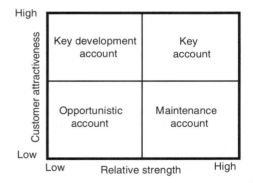

Figure 9.1 KAISM matrix for a balanced portfolio

Any business seeking a balance of present performance and future development will want accounts in all three boxes. And the bottom left? Well, when the boss calls for an impossible hike in sales by the end of the quarter, set your best hunter sales people on the customers down here – and keep them well away from the key accounts!

CROSS-FUNCTIONAL ALIGNMENT

Selection will be a rather academic exercise (and it involves far too much effort to allow it to be that) if in the end it makes no difference. The difference we are seeking is the appropriate application of business resources to the opportunities identified, and the one thing above all else that will make this difference is having the *whole* business aligned behind the selection.

The business will have to devote extra resources to the key and development key accounts. Individuals from support functions will be increasingly involved with customers, with all the implications on their workload and their objectives. Projects denied to other customers will be sanctioned for these favoured few. And just as importantly, service levels and management processes will have to be changed for those not designated as key.

None of this will happen without a cross-business alignment. Support functions will be very reluctant, and rightly so, to act in a way that looks to them like stealing from Peter to pay Paul without knowing the reason, and the ambition.

Identification without cross-business agreement will have been a long and fruitless labelling exercise

Waiting until this point, Step 9, to think about this is obviously rather late. Of course, we haven't made this mistake, indeed, we acted to avoid this back at Step 3 by assembling a cross-functional team. This team, if they have been encouraged to do so, will have been spreading the word throughout the process, paving the way to a more ready acceptance of the outcome. (One sure way to discourage such evangelism is to demand data from people without saying why you need it, particularly if it takes them some time and effort to gather, but of course you would never do such a thing.)

Having paved the way, now we must communicate to all involved the outcome, and indeed the process and the criteria that took us to this outcome. Don't expect full and immediate support for your outcome – there may still be some persuading to do, and there may still be some valuable insights to hear and take account of – but the more openly you discuss the how and the why, as well as the end result, the more likely it is that you will win support.

Using the change equation

Communication is always easiest if the audience wants to hear, so you had best start by considering if you have given them good reason to listen. What if all is well? Their department is running smoothly, customers appear to be happy, why the need all of a sudden for fancy new titles, or worse, actual *change*?

The problem here is that we are missing the first stage in the all-important process of managing change, illustrated in Figure 9.2 as the change equation. On the whole, most of us are not all that keen on change and to be persuaded not only to accept it but to actively take part in its implementation we need to have some level of dissatisfaction with how things are right now – dissatisfaction with the status quo.

But simply being thoroughly depressed is not enough, and too much depression will cause people to freeze rather than listen. We also need a shared vision of how things could be. Note the word

Don't forget your selling skills just because this is an 'inside' audience – it's now you need them most of all!

Dissatisfaction with the present **X** Shared vision of the future **X** First practical steps

> The cost of change – financial, personal, etc

The change equation

Figure 9.2 The change equation

'shared'. You have just been spending weeks or months building your vision. Your audience may have been looking in an entirely different direction, so take it easy. Of course, the more care you took at Step 3, forming the team, the less likelihood there will be of encountering diametrically opposed views at this step.

Visions are big things and sometimes they are hard to get to grips with on a practical level, so what we need are some first practical steps, some means of getting things rolling.

All of this has to be greater than the cost of change or people will simply dig their heels in and resist for all they are worth.

Managing by objectives

Once selected, cross-functional teams will be assembled to work on the key accounts. Members of these teams will develop customer-specific objectives that might go beyond their brief as a member of a function or department. At this point conflicts will occur.

Some argue that the objectives placed on an individual as a member of a key account team, when taken back into their own function, with all the conflicts that this might cause, will in itself help to

Get all functions to include key account specific objectives in their lists

seed the changes required in those functions. By such a process comes alignment, in time. This can of course be so, but you must consider firstly, whether you have the time for this kind of 'evolution', and secondly, you can in the meantime accept the conflicts that such a survival-of-the-fittest contest will breed.

Perhaps the answer is to ensure that it is not just within the key account teams that customer-specific objectives are set. Each supporting function or department must sign on to some form of customer-specific objectives. Notions of all customers being equal (just about as unhelpful as the ludicrous idea that the customer is always right) will need to be replaced with clear definitions of who is to get what, and why. To expect anyone to accept this kind of change to their work practices without having first had the opportunity to understand the process and purpose of key account selection is to open yourself up to every objection and counter-argument in the book, not to mention the subversive and clandestine wrecking tactics of the disgruntled rebels that you have created.

COMPLICATIONS

The very process of identification and selection may raise some issues not previously considered, or that were lurking there all the time, just waiting to get you.

Should we tell the customer?

KAM is very much an outward-facing process, it happens in front of the customer, but there is one aspect that you might consider keeping to yourself – the labels: key account, key development account, maintenance account, opportunistic account.

Telling key accounts that they are such is one thing, but how about being told you are in 'maintenance', or are viewed 'opportunistically'? And what in any case do you hope to gain by telling the key accounts? Their expectations will be raised and you may yet be some way off making any positive impact. This has to be one of those 'it depends' issues, and there are perhaps as many cases where telling your key accounts just what you think of them will result in a big leap forward in trust and loyalty as there are where the result will be suspicion or frustrated hopes.

Key accounts and multiple business unit suppliers

An interesting challenge for KAM is that situation where the supplier is formed into a number of business units, each working independently of the other, but selling to the same customers. Let's say a packaging company, divided into business units focused on different packaging solutions and materials, has common customers that use a variety of these solutions and materials.

Getting the message across multiple business units

Who is a key account here, and who has responsibility for them?

Business unit Alpha makes hi-tech plastic film, and its No. 1 key account – let's call them 'X' – is designated so because their business is developing fast in the pre-packed, pre-cooked food industry, where such hi-tech films are going to be of increasing importance.

Business unit Beta makes corrugated cardboard boxes, and it also sells to customer X, but not in particularly large quantities.

Is customer X defined as a key account for business unit Beta? Probably not.

Is there scope for 'difficulty' here?

Absolutely.

What if business unit Beta, having defined customer X as one of its 'opportunistic' accounts decides to let go a piece of business with X? Perhaps, worse than that, it has to let X down in order to meet the demands of one of its key accounts?

How does business unit Alpha feel about this?

Well, maybe business unit Alpha is so separate from Beta that it doesn't even realize what has happened. So no problem? What if customer X, frustrated by the poor regard the supplier holds them in, chooses to take out their frustration on business unit Alpha?

Plenty of scope for 'difficulties'.

One 'solution' is to insist that any one business unit's key accounts must be regarded as the same by all other units. Seems logical, but just wait for the fights to start.

There is a larger question: does the supplier have anything to gain by acting more in concert? The answer to this will come primarily from the customer's perspective. Does the customer buy film and corrugated card, or does it buy packaging solutions? If it is the latter, then a concerted approach will be favoured.

Global key accounts

A similar problem can result where an international business identifies a customer as a 'global' key account, but perhaps the people operating in different countries or territories take different views as to just how important this customer really is.

If the customer operates in a truly global manner, expecting uniform service from its suppliers wherever they may be, then a concerted global approach will be important. This is not always the case, however, and international businesses may still require a good deal of local variation. The only advice can be – keep you ear to the ground, be aware of shifts from local to global behaviour, or vice versa, and make sure your global organization responds appropriately.

An enthusiastic, ambitious and highly capable but entirely UK-based key account manager once had the training course of his life, only it was played out in the real world, not the classroom. He sold decorative paint, and BP was one of his key accounts, in the UK. Having seen a rather steady pace of business for some years, a new opportunity arose that was set to catapult this key account manager to stardom – BP decided to change their corporate colour scheme.

Getting the message across all territories…

A magnificent package of colour matching, premium products and top-class service was drawn up with impressive schedules for completing the changes across all UK locations within a week. The package promised some very handsome margins for the supplier, as well as a very satisfied customer.

At this point the key account manager sent some letters to their colleagues in France, Germany, Spain, Italy and the Benelux, where the same colour scheme switch was to take place, saying 'Please implement this package – details attached'. Letters came back by return, mostly saying the same thing – 'Who's BP?'. Outside the UK the company was not an important client for this paint supplier and it was now far too late to argue the case. The opportunity was lost, as was the UK business, because BP wanted one European supplier to manage the whole task.

… or not, in this case!

Leaving it to Step 9 is too late in such global customer circumstances. If you have global customers, or potential global customers, then a consideration of the implications of this on the selection process must enter the frame back at Step 1 – why are you doing all this in any case? I know of one global supplier of management consultancy services that has identified what it calls its 'crown jewels', a list of global key accounts that should be treated as such in all territories whatever the local assessment of their importance might be.

Application exercise

Plan your communications strategy:

- Who needs to be informed?
- When is the right time to start the message rolling? Is leaving it until Step 9 too late? Might starting it earlier cause confusion and disruption?
- Do you have the elements of the change equation (see above) in place?

Dissatisfaction with the status quo

- What problems might your audience be aware of?
- Are they problems that impact on their work?
- Will you need to prepare evidence of problems?

Shared vision

- What vision might your audience already have?
- Does it oppose your own vision?
- Does their vision need challenging? (Take care.)
- How might you combine the two? (Always preferable.)

First practical steps
- How can you engage their active support? – Perhaps by asking them for data or advice, or by getting them even more fully involved in the process.

The cost of change
- Do you know how this change will affect your audience?
- What will it cost them?
- What can you do to reduce that cost?

Step 10

Review, review, review

Step 10 needs the least explanation of all the steps in this process.

Keep on doing it.

Nothing is carved on tablets of stone, not even the names of key accounts. Times change and so must your KAISM analysis. One of the hardest things to do as time marches on is to start reducing the amount of resources given to a customer who once met the criteria of key account, but for whatever reason has now ceased to do so – but it must be done. Customers decline, markets become mature, people leave, companies get bought and sold – there are a dozen or more reasons and you must be ready to react appropriately.

Then of course there are those new names that emerge, and keeping your eye on these will be vital to your future. If you look at your current list of key customers and then look back to when each of them appeared on your radar screen, and why, and how, you will often find that at some point in time they were a surprise, but that somebody clung on to them because they thought that they represented the future – and as you now know, they were right.

Aim to repeat this whole process at least once a year, or more often if you are in a fast-changing market or industry – like telecommunications. Imagine you were a supplier to the telecoms industry, 20 years ago, targeting the manufacturers of consumer equipment. Would you honestly have regarded Nokia as a key or key development account? Nokia was a little known Finnish company majoring in wood pulp and rubber. If you only conduct the KAISM exercise once every five years or so, that is when surprises, like Nokia, become surprises.

The fact that there is so little to say about Step 10 should not diminish its importance. Without continual review a lot of good and hard work will become increasingly meaningless, and worse, increasingly damaging to your business. Making plans with old and outdated knowledge can often be worse than making plans with no knowledge at all!

Remember, this is a process that finishes 'some time never'

11

Next steps…

The focus of this book has been on the identification of key accounts, not the management of those accounts. The two must of course go hand in hand, and in the real world they don't always proceed in the most logical order – there are important accounts to be managed whether you have got round to calling them key or not!

The purpose of this short section is to help you consider what activities might be ahead as you develop thoughts on the selection process, so helping you to move on to the next steps.

MARKETING PLANS AND SEGMENTATION

Step 5 gave a very brief summary of the task of market segmentation. For more help with this vital activity, or to help ensure that your key account strategy fits within your business and marketing plans, *Key Marketing Skills: A complete action kit of strategies, tools and techniques for marketing success*, by Peter Cheverton, published by Kogan Page, 2000, will provide you with practical guidance.

SOFTWARE PACKAGES

Selecting key accounts can be done manually, with paper and pen, or you might prefer to use a software package. There are several available from 'quick and dirty' through to what we might call 'the full monty'. Each might fulfil a different need, whether it is a means of doing the maths, a need to compare and contrast different scenarios, or simply the desire to look professional. You can get advice on this by contacting INSIGHT Marketing and People, details below.

MANAGING KEY ACCOUNTS

The essential guide to the complexities of managing key accounts is *Key Account Management: A complete action kit of tools and techniques for achieving profitable key supplier status*, 2nd edition, by Peter Cheverton, published by Kogan Page, 2001.

This book will take you through the essential steps: how to establish and manage the right kind of relationships, how to direct a complex team sell, how to identify, understand and penetrate the customer's decision-making processes, and how to develop genuinely value-added propositions. There is also a particular focus on understanding the purchasing revolution and the customer's perspective – the all-important matter of being regarded as a key supplier.

In addition the book will help you clear the way within your business for the practice of key account management; identifying the obstacles and outlining the main requirements for success, including organizational structures, skills and systems.

The book also comes with a free CD ROM containing the INSIGHT KAISM software package.

TRAINING AND CONSULTANCY

In-house work

The advice given in this book has been tried and tested through work with the wide range of clients of INSIGHT Marketing and People. INSIGHT is an international training and consultancy firm specializing in key account management. Particular expertise has been developed through working with clients in industries and markets as diverse as pharmaceuticals and management consultancy, FMCG and telecommunications, financial services and speciality chemicals, and IT and government. The growing importance of global key accounts has found us working with the same client in Europe,

Asia Pacific, the Americas and Africa – another fund of expert experience.

The focus is on the practical application of key account strategies within businesses. This includes gaining commitment to the KAM process at the most senior level, working with clients to assess the potential benefits and opportunities, identifying the obstacles to progress, and identifying the requirements for implementation. INSIGHT can also help clients to identify their key accounts and to create and develop their key account teams.

We would be delighted to hear about your own company's specific requirements, whether they be for consultancy, facilitation of any part of the process, or tailored in-house training.

The key account excellence Performance Map©

The *Performance Map©* is a rigorous diagnostic tool (software supported) that will help you to evaluate your current level of key account excellence, and to monitor improvements as you work through your implementation plans. As well as a monitor of progress it will also highlight where your problems lie, giving you a chance to do something about them before they become insurmountable.

Figure 11.1 shows a simplified example of a *Performance Map©*.

The Masterclass

In addition to our client-specific work, we also present the INSIGHT *Advanced Key Account Management Masterclass*. The *Masterclass* is presented

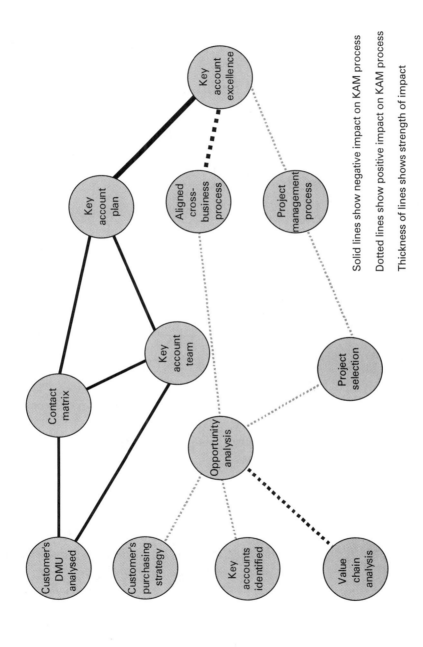

Solid lines show negative impact on KAM process

Dotted lines show positive impact on KAM process

Thickness of lines shows strength of impact

Figure 11.1 The key account excellence *Performance Map*©

at a number of international locations each year, usually including London, Brussels, Hong Kong, Singapore, New York, Johannesburg and Cape Town.

The IYSB Seminar

Identifying, selecting, and agreeing your key accounts – a 10-step process, can be delivered in-company tailored to your precise needs and circumstances.

For full details on these and other events contact INSIGHT.

CONTACT DETAILS

INSIGHT Marketing and People Ltd.
PO Box 997
Wexham Road
Slough
SL2 5JJ, UK
Tel: +44 (0) 1753 877750
Fax: +44 (0) 1753 877342
E-mail: customer.service@insight-mp.com *or*
Peter.Cheverton@insight-mp.com
Web site: www.insight-mp.com

FURTHER READING

Cheverton, Peter (2000) *Key Marketing Skills: A complete action kit of strategies, tools and techniques for marketing success,* Kogan Page, London
Cheverton, Peter (2001) *Key Account Management: A complete action kit of tools and techniques for*

achieving profitable key supplier status, 2nd edn, Kogan Page, London

Cheverton, Peter (2002) *If You're So Brilliant... How Come Your Bank Isn't Working Hard Enough?: The essential guide to developing your image and your identity*, Kogan Page, London

Haig, Matt (2002) *If You're So Brilliant... How Come You Don't Have an E-strategy?: The essential guide to doing business online*, Kogan Page, London

McDonald, Professor Malcolm (2002) *If You're So Brilliant... How Come You Don't Have a Winning Marketing Plan?: The essential guide to marketing planning*, Kogan Page, London

Index

References in italic indicate figures.